AUTOPHAGY COO[K]

EAT FOOD THAT INCREASES THE SELF-CLEANSING & AUTOPHAGY PROCESS. A SIMPLE DIET TO BUILD MUSCLE, WEIGHT LOSS AND REDUCE INFLAMMATION (METABOLIC SOLUTION)

DAN COOK

© **Copyright 2019 - All rights reserved.**

The content contained within this book may not be reproduced, duplicated or transmitted without direct written permission from the author or the publisher.

Under no circumstances will any blame or legal responsibility be held against the publisher, or author, for any damages, reparation, or monetary loss due to the information contained within this book. Either directly or indirectly.

Legal Notice:

This book is copyright protected. This book is only for personal use. You cannot amend, distribute, sell, use, quote or paraphrase any part, or the content within this book, without the consent of the author or publisher.

Disclaimer Notice:

Please note the information contained within this document is for educational and entertainment purposes only. All effort has been executed to present accurate, up to date, and reliable, complete information. No warranties of any kind are declared or implied. Readers acknowledge that the author is not engaging in the rendering of legal, financial, medical or professional advice. The content within this book has been derived from various sources. Please consult a licensed professional before attempting any techniques outlined in this book.

By reading this document, the reader agrees that under no circumstances is the author responsible for any losses, direct or indirect, which are incurred as a result of the use of the information contained within this document, including, but not limited to, — errors, omissions, or inaccuracies.

Description

Introduction

Chapter 1 The Benefits of Autophagy

Chapter 2 How to Activate Autophagy

Chapter 3 Optimizing Autophagy

Chapter 4 Water Fasting and Autophagy

Chapter 5 Autophagy for Muscle Mass

Chapter 6 Autophagy and diseases

Chapter 7 Recipes

Conclusion

Introduction.

By nature, man evolved in an environment where food was scarce. As a result, man's physiology developed complex ways to keep him healthy and in top gear, even in the absence of calories. With this, man has enough strength to look for food and thrive. Not only that, there was an intricate cellular repair process that helped man heal and take care of damages from harmful chemicals, pathogens, and even excessive sunburns.

All this takes place through the process of autophagy. With limited calories in the body, the body is equipped to recycle old cells to tap energy or use them as fuel for new ones. This is a vital cleanup process that provides many health benefits and guards against cell damage that could cause life-threatening diseases like cancer.

The best way to activate autophagy is by staying away from food and exercise. However, the kind of life we live in does not make this possible, seeing that many people eat all the time. This is evident in the proportion of Americans who are obese and overweight. Being overweight is unhealthy as it comes with many adverse health conditions. Besides, eating all the time works against the cellular repair process that takes care of cancer, aging, dementia, etc. This is where autophagy comes in.

What is Autophagy?

The word autophagy is a combination of two words: auto (self) and phage in (to eat).

Hence, the literal meaning of the word autophagy is to eat oneself. This is the process by which the body gets rid of all old and broken body cells (proteins, organelles, and cell membranes) if it cannot be sustained again. It is a regulated process in the body that breaks down and reuses cellular components.

Related to autophagy is another process called apoptosis called programmed cell deaths. After some division, cells, by nature, have to die. This sounds disturbing, without a doubt, but it is a natural process to keep a man healthy.

This can be likened to a car you bought. No matter how much you love it, it will get old and degrade with time, even though over the years, it served you well and you had great memories in it. However, with time, it will start breaking down regularly, costing thousands and thousands of dollars to fix. Later, it dawns on you that the best thing is to let go of this ride, no matter the attachment you have with it. You can get a new car instead that will serve you better.

The same process happens in the body. Body cells are also subjected to the law of aging; you are better off with them dead since their useful life is exhausted.

The Science of Autophagy: Replacing Old Parts of Cells

Still using the analogy of a car, there are times you might not need to get rid of the whole car. Just a change in the battery, or gearbox, etc., could fix the problem. This also happens at the subcellular level. There are times that apoptosis (killing off entire cells) will not make sense, instead, replacing of replacing some old cells is what you should be after (autophagy).

With autophagy, the body destroys sub-cellular organelles and brings about new ones as a replacement. The body also gets rid of old cell membranes, cellular debris, and other old and useless cells. This happens by sending these cells to the lysosome, specialized organelles with special enzymes that can help break down protein.

The first time autophagy was described was in 1962. Researchers then discovered that lysosomes increased in rats when they ingested glucagon. Lysosomes help with cell destruction, and the term autophagy was coined by the Nobel Prize scientist Christian de Duve. Damaged and old subcellular cells were marked for destruction, which happened at the lysosomes.

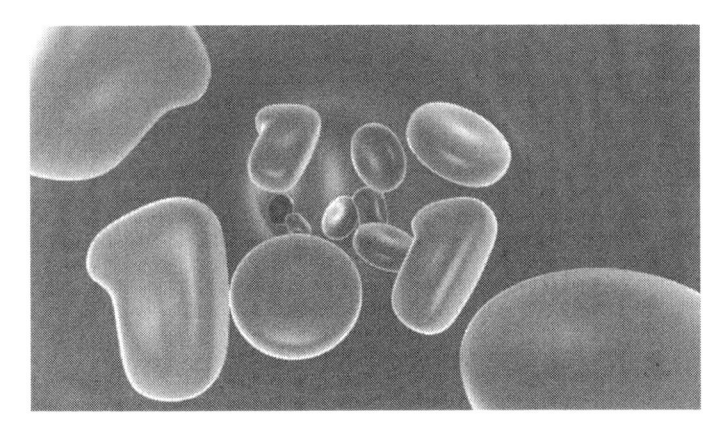

There are some important regulators of autophagy in the body. One of these is called the mammalian target of rapamycin (mTOR), a kinase. The activation of mTOR in the body suppresses autophagy; however, autophagy is promoted when mTOR is dormant.

Activation of Autophagy

The key activator of autophagy is nutrient deprivation. It is important to bear in mind that glucagon and insulin are two hormones that work in the opposite. When the level of insulin rises in the body, glucagon comes down and vice versa.

Eating makes insulin level increase while bringing down the level of glucagon. Fasting, on the other hand, reduces the insulin level, which also makes the glucagon level increase. When the glucagon level goes up, the process of autophagy gets triggered. This is why fasting (which raises autophagy) is one of the best and most potent ways to trigger autophagy.

Autophagy helps in sanitizing the cell as the body marks all old and rickety cells and their components for destruction. Without autophagy, the body accumulates all these old cells which trigger aging.

There are many health benefits of fasting, apart from autophagy. The latter part of this book will shed light on fasting, intermittent fasting in particular. Not only do you get to enjoy autophagy with fasting, but you also stimulate growth hormones. The body takes this as a clue to produce new, young, and agile body parts. You can think of this as the overhauling of a car engine.

To have a successful overhaul of a car engine, you must get rid of old and useless car engine parts before putting in new ones. With this, the process of breaking down is as vital as the process of creation. This is why fasting help reverses the aging process since old and rickety cells are being replaced with new, strong parts.

Autophagy: A Highly Controlled Process

The process of autophagy in the body is highly controlled. Too much of everything, as we are aware, could be detrimental at times. This is why it is pretty dangerous for autophagy to run out of control. In the cells of mammals, for instance, the total absence of amino acid sets the stage for autophagy, even though the separate role of each amino acid varies.

Autophagy breaks down old and useless cell components into amino acids (a form of protein). During the early hours of going without foods, the levels of amino acids start to increase. These amino acids get delivered to the liver for glucogenesis. With tricarboxylic acid as well, they can be decomposed into glucose.

Excess levels of old protein cells in the body manifest via cancer and Alzheimer's Disease (AD), which comes around as a result of excess useless proteins (Tau protein or amyloid beta), which messes up the brain. Thanks to autophagy, the body is equipped to get rid of old protein cells, which counters the development of autophagy.

Main Purpose of Autophagy in the Body

Autophagy is one of the few processes in the body that protects man against disease and germs. Unlike apoptosis, which is a death pathway, autophagy is more of a self-cannibalization pathway. With the use of lysosomal degradation, autophagy helps get rid of useless proteins and amino acids. In short, autophagy serves to maintain balance and equilibrium in body cells. Autophagy can be seen as a maintenance apparatus that keeps body cells functioning optimally by either getting rid of or recycling waste.

Autophagic Processes

There are three major ways in which the body cell gets rid of waste through the process of autophagy. These are:

Micro autophagy: occurs when the cytoplasm gets eaten up by the lysosome

Macro autophagy: concerns the formation of a double-membrane structure known as an autophagosome. This transports all cytosolic material marked for destruction into the lysosome.

Chaperone-mediated autophagy (CMA): This process selects the specific cytosolic proteins it breaks down. CMA only acts and breaks down protein with consensus peptide sequence, rather than breaking down entire organelles.

Autophagy is a normal and essential part of cell growth and development. It is important to ensure that humans have the right balance of cell content-not too much and, not too little.

There are some recognized purposes of autophagy in man. These are:

Housekeeping Function: all abnormally formed protein cells, spoiled cellular components, and damaged organelles are eliminated. The way cell autophagy takes care of the housekeeping function is through mitochondria cells and endoplasmic reticulum.

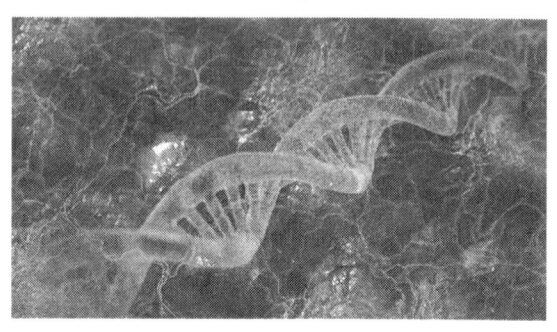

Host Defense Mechanism: somebody cells get infected by foreign toxic pathogens (disease-causing organisms). Autophagy helps eliminate such infected cells before harming the body.

Cellular Stress: In addition to getting rid of harmful body cells, autophagy acts as a response to cellular stress. Autophagy is vital as it helps bring order to the process during low body nutrients and cellular stress

Embryonic Development: By ensuring that there is a balance between the energy level and its source, autophagy ensures proper development of the embryo.

How Humans Experienced Autophagy in Times Past

The time of our forefathers was a little different from what we have today in terms of food availability. In their days, they alternated between fasting and feasting. One would think they had limited access to food, which made them starve, miserable, and wretched. Their fossil records showed quite the opposite - incredibly strong bones, powerful teeth with a very limited sign of nutritional deficiency. Besides, they did not have the luxury of strolling down to the local grocery store to exchange money for food. Their body was accustomed to going without food, which helped them enjoy autophagy.

They worked and sweated for their food. This is vastly different from what we have today where all you have to do is spend money to get access to food in varieties. They burned calories for them to get food. They tilled the ground, hunted, and were not always lucky as the animals at times, were always on guard. They climbed, chased, gathered, walked, jumped, lifted, etc., to get food.

This made it easy for their body to switch between the fed and fasted state regularly, not constantly in a fed state as it is common to us today. Since they had no trouble getting their body to a state where energy was deficient, it was easy to activate autophagy. This helped them activate and enjoy the benefits of autophagy, rather than always being in the fasted state.

Their food environment is in complete opposite to what we have today.

As long as you have money, it is practically impossible to go hungry. At every corner, you will find the tastiest and calorie-heavy foods available, even the cheapest.

No one, except the farmers and people settled in rural environments, works for their foods. All we have to do is drive to the store or even have some delivery guy bring our food items to our doorsteps. We eat hundreds and thousands of calories without any impactful physical exercise to compensate for the overload of calories.

Is Autophagy Good or Bad for Your Health?

Autophagy is a double-edged sword because it can worsen and mitigate injuries. It is important to also point to the fact that fasting enhances the onset of gallstones. This happens when bile in the gallbladder solidifies excessively. People who are pregnant, underweight, and senior citizens, etc., are not advised to fast.

As important as autophagy is, it is not always advisable.

The benefits of autophagy can be activated via the process of calorie restriction, which will be shown later. Sadly, however, there are some side effects of autophagy highlighted below:

- <u>Some tumors thrive in the presence of autophagy.</u>
- <u>There could be muscle loss with too much autophagy.</u>
- <u>Autophagy also brings about some bacterial infection.</u>

Bear in mind that when dangerous tumor cells do not get adequate calories as a result of fasting, they are stressed (Groot, 2019). Ideally, they die; however, this might not happen because autophagy works against apoptosis.

Even though autophagy seems to be a good option in the control of some diseases, it is not the best bet. Autophagy, in this case, is not good.

The summary here is that autophagy might either be good or bad, depending on some underlying conditions in the body. It is important to point out that it is not about staying away from autophagy. Rather, depending on the condition of your body, it is about getting the right and optimum amount of autophagy.

Herein lies the problem; there is no exact figure to quantify autophagy that is recommended for man. This is due to the many variables, and the fact that humans differ in numerous ways. Numerous things affect the level of autophagy you get, like your overall medical condition, your quality of sleep, relationship with food, and overall wellbeing.

There are cases where you should restrict the level of autophagy your body gets. There are stages, on the other hand, in which getting as much autophagy as possible will not pose any significant issue:

Cases of people who need more autophagy and fasting are:

- People who are overweight
- People with high inflammation
- People with high blood pressure

- <u>People addicted to eating or have other eating disorders</u>
- <u>Folks with high triglycerides</u>
- <u>Cases of people who need little autophagy and fasting are:</u>
- <u>People with cancer</u>
- <u>People with a bacterial infection</u>

Some Side Effects of Autophagy

By getting rid of inflammasome activators, autophagy helps regulate immunity and inflammation. The body also expels pathogens through autophagy in a process called xenophagy, which is essential to healthy living. When autophagy occurs, however, there are bacteria like Bartonella, Brucella, and Coxiella that multiply. These bacteria use autophagy to grow.

There is an autophagy gene called ATG6 or BECN1 which covers the Beclin1 protein. The essence of this is to act against the growth of cancer cell tumors. It has, however, been discovered that this gene is not very effective in suppressing cancer cells. The bad news is that, rather than promoting inhibiting cancer cells, it can support it through the self-replicating effect.

We recommend trying to get to autophagy as a preventive measure, rather than a treatment option. This is because the self-destruction process can energize those tumor cells, making them resilient and resistant to cancer cells. As a result, chemotherapy and starvation will do very little in getting rid of them.

All in all, it is not black and white with autophagy. It is a process that should be encouraged in the body as it destroys some viruses and bacteria. Other pathogens, however, could thrive well. Also, depending on the environment and tissues, autophagy reacts differently

Chapter 1 The Benefits of Autophagy

After a relatively daunting scientific explanation about what autophagy is and the different types of autophagy that exist, let's take a break and look at what the actual benefits are to activate it.

1. It helps in the fight against cancer.

Autophagy helps us to survive when our body is in starvation mode. Scientific research tells us that cancer was one of the primary diseases associated with autophagy; however, the way in which it works with cancer cells and the role autophagy has in them is still mostly unknown. In the advanced stages of the development of a tumor, it could help cancer cells survive under low-oxygen and low-nutrient situations.

Autophagy, most importantly, plays a role in how cancer responds to therapy. The reason being is that most cancer therapies create damage and stress to the cells to kill them. This makes a treatment that uses autophagy as a potentially good or potentially bad solution. It also depends on the type of cancer. We also have to consider what stage the disease is in and what type of autophagy and the duration of it. A few studies have revealed that increased autophagy leads to the resistance of both chemotherapy and radiotherapy, but a few others revealed that a slew of anticancer drugs helps to stimulate autophagy-oriented cell death within cancer cells.

Autophagy is clearly becoming a place of interest in clinical research as some of the more recently approved anti-cancer stratagems noted as inducing autophagy. Learning more about this can help with creating medications and radiation treatments that can aid in getting rid of tumors.

We have to be careful when looking at the way autophagy affects someone with cancer because there have been some research results that tell us that it can go into various, somewhat unpredictable manners. This makes autophagy quite the mysterious entity, but we can't ignore that it has had some promising results.

Autophagy has been linked with cancer and other illnesses such as Parkinson's disease. Currently, medical processes using the recent discoveries of Ohsumi are now happening around the world. The vital role that it plays in chemotherapeutic drugs and radiation is growing. Research shows that there are four different functional forms of autophagy which can happen when the body is responding to chemotherapy or radiation. They are: cytostatic, cytotoxic, non-protective, and cytoprotective. None of them have a specified result that scientists can predict yet. The line between protecting cancer and tumor cells and autophagy deleting them is still quite blurred. Some scientists suggest that this is where next to put research focus.

2. It can improve your cognition and the health of your brain

Inducing autophagy or fasting can also help to reduce oxidative stress in the brain by both stimulating the elimination of broken molecules and arousing the creation of endogenous antioxidants. Overall, this means that autophagy can help impact your brain's performance. The science behind autophagy and illnesses is still somewhat new, but some research shows that it can help to reduce the neuronal dysfunction that comes with diseases like Parkinson's and Alzheimer's.

3. It can help reverse and slow down aging markers.

Aging, from the scientific perspective, can be defined as the slow but overtime noticeable accretion of organelles and proteins in our cells. This can lead to the eventual death or dysfunction of cells. Consider autophagy to be an aging reversal, as it helps to give your body a cellular jumpstart. It stimulates your cells to get rid of parts of cells that are no longer needed and helps your body continue to create new cells. These cells are critical because they are the ones that help stave off things like cancer.

4. It can help improve your body's composition.

We live in a world where calorie intake is what we're told to look at almost exclusively when it comes to dieting, eating right, and watching the health of bodies; however, that's not always the case. While calories are necessary, we can't forget that body composition is based on our hormonal state.

Inducing autophagy can help increase our adiponectin levels and increase our sensitivity to insulin. Both of these are critical hormonal factors, and determine if the fat that already exists within us gets oxidized, meaning used for energy and if future caloric intake gets stored as fat or used by the body immediately. These hormonal changes are excellent, and persist after your fasting period is complete. While you will more than likely run a calorie deficit during your fasting days, the hormonal changes will have much more impact on your body's composition over the weeks and months. Yay for fasting and longevity.

One of the big myths that gym-going types have is that fasting will break down muscles for energy. There is some truth to this under dire conditions, but it's also easy to avoid if you're smart about your fasting cycle. If you do it right, short-term fasting can help increase lipolysis which is fat burning, and you can ideally maintain your muscle growth.

5. It can help improve your digestion

Instinctively, inducing autophagy is like a type of rest on your digestive system. It allows the gastrointestinal tract, also known as GI for short, to relax for a while. Ideally, this helps to produce both reduced intestinal inflammation and to help improve the contraction of the GI muscles indigestion. Collectively, they help to enhance the absorption of nutrients and aid in the quality of your bowel movements. While the research is still pretty fresh, there are hints that autophagy may help stimulate the growth of a different species of bacteria in our guts which can improve the fat burning process! This is pretty exciting!

6. It can help your cardiovascular health

Inducing autophagy can help to reduce your heart rate and blood pressure all the while raising the parasympathetic tone, which is a crucial gauge for the health of our cardiovascular systems. In the most generic terms, the strength of our cardiovascular system to form of stress improves after inducing autophagy.

Chapter 2 How to Activate Autophagy

So, the big question is: when does autophagy happen? Well, it is activated in all the cells but increases when we're in a stressful situation, such as being nutrient-deprived because of fasting or starvation. The way we activate this is to put our bodies in the process of dealing with "good stresses." Two methods of doing this are exercising, and temporarily restricting our calorie intake. Here's an extended breakdown of how we can activate autophagy.

1. Fasting.

When looking into dieting and lifestyle changes that you can learn to control, one of the things you will want to consider doing when inducing autophagy is fasting. It is one of the most effective ways of inducing autophagy. The concept of fasting is quite simple – you don't eat for a certain amount of time, though you are allowed to drink water and occasionally other liquids such as tea and coffee.

One way many people have recently started fasting is through what is called "Intermittent fasting." This is a type of fasting that encompasses time-restricted eating. IMF, as it's known for short, can be done in different forms, which will discuss later in this book. Mainly, this branched out the type of fasting that called Alternate Day fasting, which limits your daily eating window to between 4-8 hours per day and then fasting for the remainder of the day.

One of the big questions you might have right now is how long does one have to fast to initiate autophagy. Some studies have suggested that we should fast between twenty-four to forty-eight hours to have the strongest effect on our bodies. The problem with this is that is doesn't always work for everyone. It would be better to start closer to twelve to thirty-six hours at a time.

An ideal way to start is to eat just one or two meals a day instead of eating smaller meals and snacks throughout the day. If you are usually finishing up your day and having your last meal around six or seven in the evening, consider trying to fast until around seven the next morning. In more intense fasting scenarios, you can consider fasting until eleven in the morning or even twelve in the afternoon.

You can also consider occasionally doing a two to three days fast, and extend it even longer once you've adapted to fasting. If you're following the alternate day fasting, then you will be restricting your calorie intake to around 500 but then taking in enough calories that feel satiating when you're on your non-fasting days.

2. Take the Ketogenic Diet into consideration.

The ketogenic (or keto) diet is a high-fat, low carbohydrate diet that works well with fasting. Called KD for short, it involves having about seventy-five percent or more of your daily calories coming from fat, and less than five to ten percent of your calories coming from carbs. This diet thus forces your body to take on some more significant changes because your metabolic pathways shift so that you begin utilizing your body's fat for fuel instead of the glucose from carbohydrates.

Some of the foods you'll want to consider if you're going the KD route is high-fat, whole foods. Consider stuff like nuts, seeds, avocado, fermented cheeses, meat products from grass-fed animals, ghee, butter from grass-fed animals, eggs, olive oil, and coconut oil. The response from your body is fascinating. It will begin to produce ketone bodies that have protective factors in them. Some research implies that ketosis can help induce starvation-style autophagy, which also has neuroprotective functions to it. It should be noted that these are mainly from animal research, so the conclusions from these studies are far off.

3. Exercising

Recent research findings have told us that exercise helps to induce autophagy within multiple organs which are involved in metabolic regulation, like adipose and pancreas tissue, and liver and muscle tissue. The reason why exercise is considered a form of stress is that it breaks down tissues which cause them to be repaired and come back stronger once they've grown. We currently don't know the specific amount of exercise you need to do to induce autophagy, but research implies that the more intense workouts are most beneficial.

For cardiac and skeletal muscle tissue, some experts suggest as little as 30 minutes of exercising can be enough to induce autophagy. The bigger question, however, is if you can exercise while fasting. This is largely based on the individual. Some people can. Some people find that they're more energetic once they adapt to fasting, which gives them the motivation to exercise.

4. Going on a protein fast.

One fast you may want to consider if the protein fast. What you do in this fast is once or twice a week, you limit how much protein you eat by about fifteen to twenty-five grams a day. This will give you a body a full day to recycle the proteins, which can help decrease inflammation and clean your cells without the fear of muscle loss. Autophagy is triggered when the body has no choice but to feast on its own toxins and protein.

5. Performing High-Intensity Interval Training (HIIT for short).

HIIT is an excellent way to bring on autophagy. High-intensity exercise puts you in a state of "good" stress because it stresses your body out enough that you provoke a biochemical change. Your body will have just enough impact loads to make your muscles sturdier, but not enough that it will do you any harm. Some research says that you should consider approximately twenty to thirty minutes a day to give your longevity an optimal boost.

In this "less is more" type of exercise for encouraging autophagy, you'll want to consider resistance training and weightlifting exercises for about 30 minutes every other day. This is ideal for activating autophagy. The goal here is to get short-term critical stress because autophagy does well with creating stress in intervals.

6. Don't underestimate the power of restorative sleeping.

Don't forget that autophagy still happens while you're asleep as well. Take into consideration the way you sleep. There are some periods-of-sleep quizzes out there that can help you identify what type of sleep personality you have. Your sleep personality takes into account how long you sleep and in what cycles. It is crucial because understanding your sleep cycle can either enhance or ruin your day. This can help set your body up to activate autophagy through your sleep and wake cycles.

Chapter 3 Optimizing Autophagy

The right diet, exercise, fasting, and rest are something you will know when you lock onto your need for autophagy. This need could alter over time, or it may be that you don't need every aspect of it in the same way for the rest of your life. All of the research on autophagy has shown that you don't need to do it every day, but you may find times in the course of your life that you will need or want to activate it on a daily basis. You may lose all the weight you set for your goal, using all four components, but will need to adjust your approach to autophagy once that goal is reached.

Life is long and changes daily. There will never be any diet, form of exercise, or fasting ritual that has to stay the same forever unless you are practicing these experiences for religious purposes. We grow, we transform, we change, for our whole lives and so should the food we eat, the kind of exercise we get, how often we fast, and what kind of rest is best under the circumstances.

We don't have the perfect relationship with these factors in a perfect way on all days of the year; we will ebb and flow and need to understand our responsibility to ourselves to pay attention, especially if you want to use autophagy regularly to enhance your health and renewal.

Significant research on the overall impact of prolonged autophagy has not been known yet; however, many improvements are being seen and experienced in the overall health of those who include performance autophagy activation in their regular health plans.

Let your cells do the dirty work while you plan the routine, and handle the steps and instructions for initiating an autophagic response. Allow for some room to grow and shift. You don't have to follow these guidelines to a T; you can experiment and explore different ways of doing it that work best for your personal, optimal health.

Renewal is easy when you bring the right ingredients to the table. This chapter will give you the steps you need to change your diet, exercise, fasting routine, and resting time, in order to fully enhance autophagy. The four categories together promote the ideal healing platform. Remember, the recipe is in your hands, and you have the power to heal.

Right Diet

Taking what you know about how autophagy works and how to activate it, you can begin with the first important steps to creating that internal response. The next steps will give you the approach you need to shift and transition into the right diet. The right diet will initially be a keto-diet for the best autophagic response and weight loss, depending on your goals. A modified diet down the road will be beneficial as well; keeping your body healthy means listening and responding to its needs. A long-term keto diet can be adjusted to allow for more carbohydrates.

To begin a ketosis meal plan, you need to ease into it, as you would ease into a period of fasting. The reason for this is that when you immediately stop eating all the foods you are used to eating, such as bread, pasta, sugar, fruit, and many other items, you can enter a shock phase. For some, it can feel like illness, and there can be headaches, cravings, and fatigue. It can feel a lot like the flu. Your body has been eating certain foods for a while, and to suddenly deprive the body of these things can create an inflammatory response.

To create a smoother transition from your current eating habits to a keto diet, you will need to break it down into phases and allow for some time. Week 1 will be the first phase of transition, eliminating some of the foods that you need to avoid creating ketosis. Week 2 will be the second phase of further elimination and increase in fat and protein. Here is a breakdown of what that may look like:

PHASE 1: ELIMINATION

- Alcohol
- Unhealthy fats like canola oil, vegetable oil, mayo, margarine, imitation butter
- All processed, low-fat foods
- Condiments containing sugars and carbs
- Most grains, including pasta, cereal, bread. You can keep small quantities of grains during phase 1, like rice, quinoa, and barley.

During this elimination, you are taking away some significant carbohydrates but are still allowed to eat some carbs and sugars found in fruit, starchy vegetables, legumes, and other sugary foods and beverages which will prevent a significant body shock. A possible weekly diet for Phase 1 could look like this:

Monday

Breakfast: eggs and bacon with tomato and mushrooms

Lunch: Salad with salmon and fruit on the side

Dinner: Chicken soup with rice

Tuesday

Breakfast: yogurt and berries with a tsp of honey and 3tbsp of almond slivers

Lunch: BLT on whole grain bread

Dinner: Steak and potatoes with broccoli

Wednesday

Breakfast: Fruit bowl with yogurt

Lunch: Salad with chicken and quinoa

Dinner: 3 bean soup with sausage and veggies

Thursday

Breakfast: Goat cheese and basil omelet with tomatoes

Lunch: Salmon and asparagus cooked in butter and lemon

Dinner: Roast chicken with carrots and potatoes

Friday

Breakfast: Poached eggs with tomatoes and kale

Lunch: Codfish with steamed vegetables and butter

Dinner: Beef Stew

Saturday

Breakfast: Fruit and nuts

Lunch: Turkey lettuce wraps

Dinner: Roasted pork shoulder with vegetables

Sunday

Breakfast: Eggs and bacon with a spinach feta salad

Lunch: Salad niçoise

Dinner: Baked Salmon and broccoli

This weekly diet starts to prepare you for an even bigger elimination of carbs and sugars, increasing fat and protein. Cooking with healthy fats like olive oil, coconut oil, and avocado oil is encouraged in Phase 1 and should be adhered to in Phase 2. You can also cook with a small amount of butter or clarified butter known as ghee.

There are many keto-diet cookbooks that contain specific cooking recipes to help you avoid incorporating any foods that you are working to eliminate. Avoidance of alcohol during phase one is important. Your body converts alcohol into sugar, so it is like drinking glasses or pints of candy. Increase water consumption and try more herbal teas. One of the reported side effects of ketosis is bad breath. This is caused by ketones being released in the body from burning fat and can be evident in your breath. Rather than chewing sugary gum or sucking on sweet mints or lozenges, try a few cups of peppermint tea between meals. Adding freshly squeezed lemon juice to your glasses of water is a wonderful digestive aid and can help with balancing internal pH levels. You can also use apple cider vinegar in place of lemon juice to create the same effect.

Stay away from processed, packaged foods and try to prepare meals with fresh ingredients for the best results. Let go of all the protein and power bars, all the cookies and snacks, all the pastries and flavored lattes. Let go of all the bread and baked goods, all the food made with canola oil and corn syrup. This is what you begin to do in Phase 1. Give this phase some time. It doesn't have to be only one week. It may feel more comfortable for you to extend this phase into 2 weeks or more while your body adjusts. And be sure to drink plenty of water throughout.

PHASE 2: ELIMINATION

- All grains including any remaining bread, rice, quinoa, etc.
- All fruit, except small portions of berries
- All sugars and sugar additives, including honey and any beverage containing sugar
- Legumes—beans, chickpeas, etc.

- *Starchy vegetables like beets, carrots, potatoes, yams, and parsnips*

During this elimination, you are further letting go of any remaining carbs and sugars. The standard ketosis diet allows for 5% daily intake of carbs in ratio to your fat and protein consumption. You can get these carbs from berries and some quantities of vegetables.

In Phase 2, you will be incorporating more of the high fat/high protein foods your body needs to stave off hunger and cravings, allowing your body to enter enhanced stages of weight loss and ketosis. A typical weekly diet with full elimination could look like this:

Monday

Breakfast: spinach and goat cheese omelet with three eggs

Lunch: tuna salad with feta, olive oil, and lots of leafy lettuce greens

Dinner: pork chops with kale salad and broccoli

Tuesday

Breakfast: yogurt and berries

Lunch: big green salad with one avocado, cucumber, celery, green bell pepper, cabbage, toasted walnuts, and an olive oil lemon dressing

Dinner: salmon and asparagus with butter and lemon

Wednesday

Breakfast: bacon and eggs with tomato and basil, side salad

Lunch: guacamole with celery and cucumber sticks, a handful of nuts

Dinner: pesto chicken and roasted broccoli and brussels sprouts

Thursday

Breakfast: mushroom, spinach, tomato-basil omelet

Lunch: chicken salad lettuce wraps

Dinner: steak and eggs with salad

Friday

Breakfast: poached eggs on an arugula salad with feta and olive oil

Lunch: roasted pork loin and steamed veggies

Dinner: tilapia cooked in butter with sautéed broccoli, kale, and spinach

Saturday

Breakfast: yogurt and berries

Lunch: toasted nuts, one avocado, smoked salmon and celery sticks

Dinner: roasted turkey breast with a side salad

Sunday

Breakfast: omelet with scallions, mushrooms, cheddar

Lunch: salad niçoise

Dinner: roast chicken and brussels sprouts

Keep in mind that while cooking for a ketosis diet, if you need snacks between meals, eat nuts and seeds, or another kind of protein snack. Use healthy oils and clean ingredients. Do not use canned vegetables.

The Phase 2 diet has removed sugars, most carbs and increased proteins and healthy fats. Use ketosis recipes and cookbooks to help you adjust measurements based on your own weight and BMI. Additionally, if you are going to enjoy breakfast or snack items like yogurt and berries, be sure that you are choosing full-fat yogurt that does not contain any added sugars or flavorings.

Finding the right supplements for you can also improve the quality of your daily nutrient intake. Many herbal teas are packed with minerals, vitamins, and nutrients. Having a hot cup of tea between meals can stave off hunger, while soothing and warming the belly, helping it to feel full while packing in minerals and antioxidants.

Bone broth can be an excellent supplement to some meals as it is very filling and nutrient-dense. Broths can also be useful in phasing out food to begin transitioning into a fasting period. Bone broths are simple and easy to make at home. You can purchase some quality bone broths from the store, but if you are cooking chicken for your ketosis diet, you can freeze the bones until you are ready to make broth and then put them in a crockpot overnight with purified water. Add some onion and celery for flavor. There are several recipes available for broths, and you can use a variety of bones, not just chicken.

Broths are soothing to the intestinal lining, providing a healthy space for nutrient absorption. Adding bone broths into your daily meals can be a huge improvement to your quality of digestion. You can have a cup of broth instead of tea or skip breakfast or dinner and just enjoy a cup of hot broth.

Finding ways to enjoy the program your body is undertaking can feel like a challenge at first, but initiating the process is part of the pleasure of starting your journey to healing. A cup of broth or a handful of your favorite nuts can go a long way.

Every person is different, weighs a different amount, and has a different health history. Finding the right recipes for you will help you feel like you can satisfy and satiate your hunger. Ketosis diets are in full, popular swing, and there are numerous delicious recipes to keep you on the right track. Engaging in a ketosis diet while enjoying some of the other autophagic activation methods will ensure a whole healing, whole-body process.

Right Exercise

Get yourself ready to move your muscles. There isn't a time in your life when exercise will have no value or benefit. It is always a good idea to include exercise in your life. The limits of exercise depend on the person and the goals being worked toward; however, whatever exercise is chosen, you will add to the output of autophagy.

When you dial into the kind of exercise that works for your frame, build, performance goals, and intentions, you can expand on that exercise in various ways, creating the right routine for you. The key is finding something you enjoy. You don't have to program yourself to exercise like everyone else. In fact, that can cause burn out and avoidance. The right exercise is what is right for you.

Most exercise routines or plans promote some level of variety. This is essential to a balanced, physical health plan. What you choose depends on you, but within your routine, there should be a balance between resistance training or weights, cardio, balance, and stretching.

For optimal autophagy performance, there needs to flow within each of the methods. Doing the same exercise routine 6 days a week is not going to benefit anyone, long-term. Different muscle groups need time to recover and heal after the stress and strain of healthy exercise.

Here are some examples of some possible weekly workouts to promote autophagy:

EXAMPLE 1:

Monday: Calisthenic Routine
Tuesday: Yoga
Wednesday: Weights
Thursday: Rest
Friday: Calisthenic Routine

Saturday: Yoga

Sunday: Walking with weights

EXAMPLE 2:

Monday: Stretching for one hour

Tuesday: Barre/Pilates class

Wednesday: Rest and water fast

Thursday: Power walking with weights

Friday: Swimming Laps

Saturday: Rest and water fast

Sunday: Pilates

EXAMPLE 3:

Monday: Weight lifting

Tuesday: Jogging for an hour

Wednesday: Rest and 18 hours fast

Thursday: Stretching and walking with weights

Friday: Swimming

Saturday: Rest and water fast

Sunday: Yoga

There are numerous ways you can plan an exercise routine, and if you begin to feel bored with it, you can change it! You may want to have a gym membership so that you have access to the equipment, machines and swimming pool, or you may prefer a home work out set up so you can easily exercise whenever you need to. You can acquire weight sets, stretch bands, yoga mats, and medicine balls to have available for use at any time. A little a day goes a long way.

Calisthenics

A majority of people today are aware of things like yoga, running, weight lifting, and all the different types of fat-burning cardio workout you can find. Many people, though, are not as familiar with calisthenics. They are common enough exercises, but you may not have heard the name before. If you have heard of Cross Fit, then you understand calisthenics.

It is essentially a series of regular motor movements like standing squatting, walking, running, swinging, etc. that use your own body weight for resistance and strength building. You really don't need a lot of machinery or equipment to use this kind of exercise. Many gyms offer training like this, providing a variety of different movements in a routine so that your whole body gets a full work out. You can also find several online videos that can guide you through a full calisthenics' routine, many of which do not require any equipment.

Whatever method or schedule of exercise you choose, the right exercise is what is right for you, and all exercise will benefit your overall health, wellness, vitality and most importantly, autophagy.

Chapter 4 Water Fasting and Autophagy

Water fasting, even though it is a fast, differs from intermittent fasting. This is because water fasting involves staying away from food and drinks entirely for a given period, the duration of the fast. In other words, you only drink water to suppress hunger throughout the fast. Water fasting can range from 24 hours to 72 hours, depending on what you want. It is, however, not recommended that you exceed 72 hours.

Worthy of note is the fact that people should be careful before starting a water fast. The advice of an expert, such as a dietician or doctor, is vital before attempting a water fast. People fast for many reasons. Two of the most important reasons are to shed off excess fat and detoxify the body (autophagy).

As indicated above, when you fast, you go without food for hours or days depending on what you want. The intention is to induce autophagy.

Pregnant women, people with chronic kidney issues, as well as people with a history of eating disorders should not try water fasting. This is because of the intensity of the fast and the limitations it places on individuals. We recommend a maximum of 72 hours due to the side effects that could arise from fasting. If you would like to extend the fast, the advice of a doctor is non-negotiable. Besides, you can consider retreat centers that offer fasting programs where you are under the constant supervision of health practitioners where you can be easily supported.

Worthy of note is the fact that you should not stress your body too much while trying water fasting because of the side effects associated with it. You might not be able to escape dizziness and lightheadedness on the fast, especially if you're a first-timer.

All in all, make sure you avoid driving or operating heavy machinery while on a water fast. The next part explores the benefits and side effects of water fasting.

Water Fasting Pros

There are many reasons why people fast. It could be for religious or health reasons. If you are going to undergo a surgery in the hospital, for instance, you will have to stay away from food. This shows that there is something special about fasting and health. Fasting comes in many forms. Water fasting, unlike other types of fasting, is highly restrictive because you get zero calories and no food at all. You have to be determined and mentally prepared, as it is not going to come on a bed of roses. With that aside, many health benefits come with water fasting. This part of the book will shed light on these.

Cell Regeneration or Autophagy

Since the theme of this book is autophagy, I believe it is okay to start with autophagy as one of the health benefits of water fasting. Cellular regeneration is one of the main advantages of water fasting. Also known as autophagy, it is the natural ability of the body to get rid of dysfunctional cells. Water fasting forces the body to go into an induced state of autophagy. What happens is that the body will have to choose which cells are relevant and functioning, to keep them protected, and also ensure they get adequate nutrients, since nutrient intake is limited already.

At the same time, the body disposes of old cells that are no longer relevant in the body. It also creates new, durable, and healthy body cells as a replacement for the ones disposed of. The ability of the body to get rid of these damaged body cells and replace them with new, healthy ones improves the healing capacity of the body.

Slows Down Aging

You not only get to enjoy autophagy with water fasting. Many other tremendous health benefits come with water fasting, one of which is slowed down aging. When there is an excess supply of oxygen in the body, it triggers an abundance of free radicals, which results in cellular oxidation, which also causes premature aging.

When you go into water fasting, however, the body cells already damaged by free radicals get expelled. This makes way for new, young, and healthy body cells, which translates to looking and feeling young. Bear in mind that when you expel old body cells, you make the body stronger, with a renewed capacity to fight off disease, infections, and germs. Hence, it is more than just aesthetic as some may think. Besides, new body cells can communicate with each other better to keep the body healthy.

Weight Loss

Generally, it is expected that when you stay away from food for a given period, the body goes into ketosis. It is usually not until you eat the ketogenic diet that you get into ketosis. The body goes into ketosis because no more food is coming in; hence, it is forced to turn on its reserve – fats. It derives energy from fats stored in the body and breaks them down.

Thus dieting, as well as water fasting, can get you into ketosis, which leads to the burning of fat. You, however, need to know that ketosis makes the body draw needed energy from body fat. As a result of this, you have to be careful about the activities you do during water fasting due to the restricted calorie intake. Feeling lightheaded is common during water fasting partly thanks to ketosis.

Improved Insulin Receptivity

The pancreas creates a hormone called insulin, which helps keep the blood sugar level of the body in check. When you fast, the body gets better at controlling spikes in glucose levels. Not only that, but the body can also send these hormones to keep the blood sugar level from rising. Since the body becomes more sensitive to insulin, there is a lower risk of developing diabetes now or later in life.

Reduced Risk of Cancer and Heart Disease

There is evidence to support the fact that water fasting does help reduce the risk of cancer and heart disease. This is not surprising, as this benefit of water fasting is the offshoot of cell cleansing (autophagy) and reduced inflammation.

Also, there is evidence to support the fact that water fasting may slow or even completely stop the growth of tumors. Not only that, but it also improves the effectiveness of chemotherapy while helping to reduce the side effects. As a result, cancer treatment, when combined with water fasting, gives terrific results.

Also, as indicated above, water fasting helps get rid of free radicals in the body. This keeps the heart protected from any damage that might come from free radicals.

Reduced Blood Pressure

To reduce blood pressure, health practitioners advised limiting salt intake and increasing water intake. This is the basis of water fasting. Hence, it automatically helps manage and reduce blood pressure. Even people with hypertension can show significant improvement if they water fast under medical supervision.

Possible Side Effects of Water Fasting

As emphasized above, water fasting is highly restrictive. Hence, it does come with several side effects that you should note. This will help you decide if it is worth exploring or not. Also, it is essential I drive home the fact that the water fast is best and safer with the supervision of a medical practitioner. This is because they will be more equipped in helping to manage the associated side effects.

With the above in mind, expect and be prepared for the following when going on a water fast.

Dehydration

This is somewhat ironic; I must admit but bear in mind that the possibility of getting dehydrated is high while on a water fast. This is because the body gets some percentage of its water in the food ingested; however, water fasting restricts you from any form of food at all.

This is why dehydration is possible with water fasting as well. As a result, an increased amount of water intake is essential during a water fast. Keep in mind that with dehydration, the chances of feeling lightheaded and dizzy also increase.

Unintended Weight (Muscle) Loss

It is the loss of fat in the body that translates to weight loss. Although fat also serves as energy reserves in the body, it has no other use in excess amounts. One bad thing about water fast is that the body loses muscle weight, which is not good. This is because muscle is vital to keep the metabolism active even while resting, keeping the body from shock.

Muscle also helps as you go about your day to day activities. However, since the body has no access to calories while water fasting, you will not only lose shape fast but lose muscle weight as well.

Heartburn and Stomach Ulcers

The intake of food to the stomach is paused. This causes the digestive system to go on a break. Stomach acid with no purpose can trigger stomach ulcers and heartburn. The possibility of this is high, especially if you have had it in the past.

However, adequate water intake is a way to help reduce the impact of stomach ulcers and heartburn.

There are other side effects, but these are the basics. Bear in mind that one of the easiest ways to induce autophagy is via water fasting. It even proves faster than exercise or other means. This is why we thought to explore water fasting in detail.

Getting Started With Water Fasting

The best and safest way to go about water fasting is with the help of a doctor. Their expertise is significant in guiding you on what to expect and also to mitigate the associated side effects. Also, should any health conditions arise as a result of the fast, you will be able to manage with ease.

When fasting, planning is vital. If you have never fasted before, it is not recommended to jump into three days of water fasting. That is not ideal. As effective as water fasting is, if done improperly, it could cause more harm than good. This is why you have to plan well.

What to Expect During a Water Fast

The period of water fasting is a time to rest, not stress your body in any form. Since there is no calorie intake coming in, you should strive to preserve the little energy reserve your body uses to survive. Therefore, this is not the time to go out partying or exercising strenuously - instead, you need to sleep. Your body needs it. Be sure to listen to the demands of your body and give in to more sleep to compensate for the deprived energy. Sleep during the day and get 10 hours or more of sleep at night. This is nothing out of the ordinary. Embrace and enjoy the process.

Be sure to concentrate on taking in at least 2 liters of water per day. Of course, you are not drinking all this at once. Instead, you drink it throughout the day to keep yourself hydrated.

Water fasting comes with many health benefits; however, it will not come on a platter of gold, as the first couple of days will be tough. There will be unpleasant symptoms such as irritability, disorientation, and extreme hunger. The good news, however, is that you have a healthy body that can adapt fast. By the third day, you should feel much better.

When on water fast, it is essential you plan your schedule. We advise staying off work for the period of the fast. Or better still, schedule your fast for the weekend if time off will be impossible. Also, chose the fasting duration you want. If you are a beginner, we recommend a day or a maximum of three days.

Concentrate More on High-Quality Water

Fresh, clean, and high-quality water is the best to consume while on a water fast. Should the water you drink be laden with impurities, you will see the side effects quickly as the absence of food rapidly magnifies this. With the above in mind, be sure to concentrate only on distilled water while on your water fast. Filtered or boiled water is also a good idea.

It is important to reiterate that fasting is not for pregnant or lactating mothers. Nutritional deficiencies might hurt a developing child. Also, people with type 1 diabetes should not go for water fasting. People who are underweight as well should try other means to induce autophagy, rather than water fasting. If you have less than 20 pounds you want to lose and you want it to go fast, be sure you don't follow a protracted fast.

If you are determined and ready to go on with water fasting, make sure you proceed with caution and the right mindset.

Final Thoughts

We have introduced water fasting as one of the most efficient ways of inducing autophagy. Water fasting is an extreme form of fasting that comes with side effects, but tremendous health benefits. Water fasting will get you into autophagy faster than exercise and calorie restriction. However, water fasting needs to be regulated and controlled. Extended durations of fasting are best done under the supervision of a doctor.

Chapter 5 Autophagy for Muscle Mass

Autophagy is just as useful for preserving muscle as it is at for losing weight. This is part of what makes autophagy-dependent programs a lifestyle rather than merely a diet. In stimulating autophagy through fasting, dieting, or exercise you create a new paradigm for your body that triggers a series of changes that lead to an entirely new health outlook. Men and women who experience fatigue, a weakened immune system, and obesity can suddenly find that they are losing weight, more energetic, and less prone to colds than they had formerly been. And all of this is due to finding ways of incorporating autophagy stimulation into their lives.

As you have already seen, activating autophagy is as simple as remembering three simple words: dieting, fasting, and exercise. We can also add a fourth word – food – but technically this is part of dieting. Dieting and food also allow you to improve your metabolism, which will not only lead you to look better and feel better but to have more energy and longevity. Some even describe a glow that people have because of autophagy. This is not pseudoscience. Autophagy has been shown to provide benefits to skin, hair, and other organs: all as a result of the improved functioning of the body that results from careful and considerate stimulation of this process.

Some of you may be wondering what autophagy can possibly have to do with working out and muscle mass. It has everything to do with it, to be honest. Autophagy improves your metabolism, increases your insulin sensitivity, and burns fat through direct lipolysis. These are all things that men and women interested in building muscle, or merely in looking better and losing weight, hope to achieve. Stimulation of autophagy pathways is essential to anyone looking to improve their bodies by adding muscle without having to resort to illicit performance-enhancing drugs.

Intermittent Fasting

This is a convenient juncture to begin the discussion of intermittent fasting, one of the most popular diets in the health and fitness industry right now. Indeed, intermittent fasting is popular even outside the fitness industry as many men and women have discovered how this diet can dramatically alter their bodies and their lives. Intermittent fasting has the term fasting in it, but it really out to be thought of as a type of diet. This is because, in intermittent fasting, one of the most important things that the dieter needs to do is to learn to pay attention to macronutrients as well as total caloric intake.

Indeed, it is a myth in both the Ketogenic diet and intermittent fasting that the total amount of calories consumed is unimportant. Although some people who consume high caloric diets as part of their sport – like professional athletes, bodybuilders, and powerlifters – might pay less attention to their calories than others would this does not mean they are unimportant. In intermittent fasting, it is important to pay attention to the total number of calories consumed in a day and when you are consuming them as part of keeping track of your macronutrients (or macros) and in order to make sure that you are eating enough in order to meet your respective macro needs for the day.

In other words, in intermittent fasting, you have to pay attention to calories or risk finding yourself hungry because you did not properly estimate how much you need to eat during your eating window. This brings us to a discussion of what precisely intermittent fasting is and how it works. Intermittent fasting is essentially what it sounds like. It is a diet (or eating program) that involves a period of fasting separated by periods of eating. The duration of the fasting period can vary based on the specific regimen adopted by the dieter. Intermittent fasting is usually divided into two types:

- Alternate-day fasting
- Time-restricted eating

These are similar. They only differ in terms of whether the fasting lasts for an entire day or part of the day. In alternate-day fasting, the dieter spends an entire day (24 hours) without eating, while in time-restricted feeding the day is divided into periods of eating and fasting. Both alternate-day fasting and time-restricted feeding are popular ways of going about this diet with men and women finding ways of making the eating schedule work in their often hectic lives.

Time-restricted feeding, however, has received more attention from the health and fitness media because it has attracted a number of influential supporters in the community. This type of diet is popular for bodybuilders and fitness competitors who are looking to shed fat and preserve as much muscle as possible. Although calories are important and need to be planned carefully, this type of diet can allow you to consume high calories as long as they are within a certain window.

So how does the time-restricted feeding type of intermittent fasting diet work? It is pretty simple. The dieter comes up with a particular window in hours that they will be allowed to eat in the day and fasts for the rest of the day. A popular type is the so-called 16/8 split. This protocol involves consuming all of your meals in an 8-hour window and fasting for the remaining 16 hours.

This would take the form of eating, say, between 11 AM and 7 PM (an 8-hour window) and fasting the rest of the day. This split has been shown to be very effective at shedding fat, but you can use whatever window you choose. It can be a 20/4 window, in which you only eat for four hours in the day, or it can be more or less restrictive.

It also has some benefits of its own. These have been elucidated by vigorous study both inside the fitness community and outside of it. The benefits of intermittent fasting are numerous. Here are some of them:

- **Improved fat loss**
- **Improved cardiovascular functioning**
- **Improved glucose control**
- **Increased lifespan**
- **Reduced muscle loss**
- **Reduced hunger**
- **Improved metabolism**
- **Improved self-image and energy**
- **Reduced risk of cancer**
- **Reduced risk of neurodegenerative disease**

Incorporating Intermittent Fasting into Your Workout Plan

If you have an active workout regimen (or an active life), it is important to choose a diet that works with your workout and other responsibilities. Fasting is difficult for many people because they feel they need the calories that come from food for their occupation, their workout regimen, or just for the energy to get them through a day filled with screaming children or obnoxious bosses and coworkers. There is nothing wrong with that. Intermittent fasting can allow you to have shorter periods of "fasting" in your day so you are able to eat as you need.

The key is to come up with a schedule that fits with your life. For example, if you need to be at work at 8 AM and you typically go to the gym at 6 AM, perhaps you should consider a 16/8 intermittent fasting split with an eating window between 7:30 AM and 3:30 PM. This will allow you to squeeze your eating period into your busy day. For those whose obligations are later in the day, you may want to push your eating window back a little so that you are not engaging in heavy activities on an empty stomach.

Little side notes about eating before a workout: many fitness enthusiasts have found advantages to working out on an empty stomach. Although your energy levels may be slightly reduced at first because you are used to having sugar constantly in your bloodstream, it has been shown that working out on an empty stomach increases your metabolism, improves insulin sensitivity, and provides a host of other benefits. Consider working out on an empty stomach if you work out first thing in the morning. You could always have your first meal in your window after your workout.

Other things to keep in mind here will be touched on in the Frequently Asked Questions section. Some are curious about what they should eat before a fast, after a fast, or whether it is safe for them to fast. These questions and many more will be answered. All you have to do is keep reading.

Foods that Stimulate Autophagy

Most of you reading this book are likely doing so not because you plan on writing a paper and submitting it to a journal. Most likely you have a specific goal that you plan to achieve with Autophagy and you are looking for tools to help you achieve that goal. Your goal may be weight loss, it may reduction in cancer risk, or it may just be feeling better through dieting or fasting. If any of these are your goals, thinking about the sorts of food you should eat is clearly something that would be beneficial to you.

In this chapter, we will review some of the major foods that have been shown to stimulate autophagy. We will choose several foods to explore in detail. So what are the foods that you can incorporate into your diet in order to stimulate autophagy? Some of the major foods in this category include:

- **Ginger**
- **Green tea**
- **Reishi mushrooms**
- **Turmeric/curcumin**

These foods each stimulate autophagy although they do it in different ways. Some readers may notice that several foods on this list are regarded as superfoods that provide a wide host of benefits. These are foods that are consumed in some traditional cuisines, especially in East Asia and South Asia. These are areas where residents most likely identified early on that these superfoods provided benefits for health and longevity, even if they may not have understood why exactly in these early days.

You may be asking yourself how you can incorporate these foods into your diets. Some of these, like green tea, are easily incorporated. Drinking one to two glasses of green tea in the first half of your day is not difficult to do. It might be a better idea to drink tea in the first portion of your day because the caffeine in your tea can keep you up at night. There are also are some particular aspects of green tea to keep in mind (which will be explored shortly). Ginger and Reishi mushrooms are ingredients that can be conveniently added to a wide variety of dishes, such as salads or soups. Turmeric/curcumin is a dry spice that also can be added to meat dishes or a wide variety of other dishes. Getting a benefit from these does not require that you go overboard, although if you find that you like one or more of these and would like to add more to your mealtimes, it is generally safe to do this in the case of the four foods provided here.

Ginger

Ginger is one of those foods that are so good for you that it is difficult to overstate its power. Indeed, ginger has been shown to have dramatic anti-oxidant benefits that place it as a great resource for those dealing with an infection. Ginger has also been purported to increase longevity. This last claim should come as no surprise as research has shown that ginger directly stimulates autophagy, which will be explained further shortly. Ginger exists in the form of a thick and fragrant root. It has a characteristic odor and taste. Ginger together with honey is a traditional and very effective remedy for resolving the common cold.

For our purposes, it is important to note that ginger contains a number of important compounds. These include gingerol as well as a group of compounds known as shogaols. 6-shogoal is the most common of this group of chemicals. These chemicals are similar in structure to gingerol. 6-shogaol is believed to be the more important compound in autophagy. It has been shown to induce autophagy in cancer cells, but not programmed cell death (apoptosis). This has been shown to be particularly powerful in lung cancers. Incorporating ginger in your diet will help you boost your immune system and fight off cancer, all through the power of autophagy.

Green Tea

Many volumes have been written about tea and its benefit. Here, we focus on one of these teas: green tea. Green tea is a popular variety although it does compete for sales with some of the other varieties. Indeed green tea is just one of many different commercially available teas that have been demonstrated to provide health benefits to those who drink it. Green tea also has antioxidant properties and is believed to have anti-aging benefits. It boosts autophagy in the skin and can improve organ function, too. In fact, one should keep in mind that even if particular foods are associated with particular benefits, because they stimulate autophagy they are likely to provide some of the other autophagy benefits too (like improved metabolism) even if it is to a slightly lesser degree.

The compound that we are interested in is called EGCG. Epigallocatechin gallate, or EGCG, is a catechin found in teas. EGCG has a polyphenol structure and it is the most abundant catechin found in tea. Also contained in other foods, EGCG has been studied extensively because of its many potential health benefits. EGCG stimulates autophagy in hepatic cells leading to lipolysis, or lipid breakdown. EGCG accomplishes this by increasing the concentration of AMP-activated protein kinase. As we have seen, AMPK is a direct stimulator of autophagy

Reishi Mushrooms

Mushrooms can easily be added to many different meals. Reishi mushrooms would break a fast although it is worth it because of its autophagy benefits. Adding Reishi mushrooms to your diet has been shown to reduce the incidence of colon cancer. Reishi mushrooms do not demonstrate their effects through AMP Kinase, but through another pathway called the mitogen pathway. Reishi mushrooms have also been shown to have a role in stabilizing the nervous system. Adding this mushroom to your diet really can go a long way in helping you feel better and experience positive health outcomes.

Turmeric/curcumin

Turmeric/curcumin is a spice that is commonly found in South Asian cuisine. Indeed, in some parts of India turmeric is put in most dishes. Curcumin in turmeric does not have the best bioavailability, but this can be increased by consuming black pepper along with this orange/brown spice. Turmeric is a component of Indian Ayurvedic Medicine as are the other items in this list of autophagy stimulators. Turmeric specifically is regarded as having great neuroprotective effects and anti-inflammatory powers. Turmeric also plays an anti-cancer role through the mediation of AMPK (activating it through phosphorylation). Adding turmeric to your intermittent fasting or Ketogenic diet dishes can go a long way in further boosting the autophagy benefits you already expect.

Chapter 6 Autophagy and diseases

There have been many studies showings that autophagy can help with reducing the risk of cancer, which is why this diet is one of the best things to follow when it comes to reducing the risk of any disease that you might be facing. Many studies are showing that most people who have cancer and start the following autophagy fought off cancer and started to live a healthy life. Which is why we always recommend that you follow the autophagy when it comes to reducing the risk of cancer, or if you already have cancer, you can follow this diet to get rid of it. However, if you are facing cancer, then make sure to consult your doctor before you make any abrupt decisions.

The reason why autophagy works so well when it comes to reducing the risk of cancer is that it lowers your acidic level. When you have lower acidic levels, there's less chance of your body attracting more foul bacteria in your body which will cause cancer. This environment will discourage any cancer surviving growth, which is why many people recommend you follow autophagy. Some people might say autophagy is not the right answer when it comes to reducing the risk of cancer, in fact, most people said as long as you eat healthy foods then you will reduce the risk of cancer. However, many studies are showing that your lung and your other organs might be higher in the acidic level, which is why you're attracting more cancer in your body. The main thing you need to understand when it comes to reducing the risk of cancer is that cancer likes to thrive on acidic levels.

If your body is very acidic, you will be at a higher risk of attracting cancer regardless, which is why the autophagy works so well at reducing the risk of cancer. Moreover, people have also shown to reduce the risk of inflammation, which makes it a great idea to follow autophagy when it comes to reducing the risk of cancer. As you might or might not know, one of the main reasons why we attract cancer is the inflammation in our body. Many people get cancer because they are inflamed, and it's causing issues overall increasing the risk of cancer. Once people start losing the inflammation in the body, the risk of cancer lowers even further making it a great idea to start the following autophagy as autophagy reduces the risk of cancer and inflammation in your body. Also, as you know, autophagy has shown to rejuvenate our body. Once you start to break down your old cells and come out with new ones, your body will have more fighting power towards the cancerous cells.

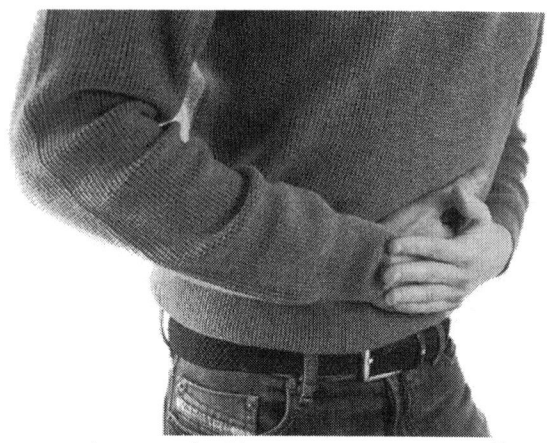

Making the autophagy one of the best diets to follow when it comes to reducing the risk of cancer. If your goal is to live a healthier life, then one of the main things you need to understand is your body recycling and detoxifying it very quickly. This is where the autophagy comes on, any time you detoxify your body will be in much better shape to get rid of any diseases more specifically cancer. Anyhow, many people go on fasts and other things to detoxify the body. This will also come in handy when it comes to reducing the risk of cancer, but the way these diet works is so perfectly that does not only detoxify your body but also makes it an autophagy environment where bacteria which because cancer cannot survive. Also, when you are eating these high autophagy foods, you're not only making it better for yourself to reduce the risk of cancer. You are also making your body more bacteria-friendly, as you will be adding more good bacteria in your body, helping you fight off the harmful bacteria in your body. As you might know, we have two types of bacteria in our body, and we have the good ones and the bad ones. We ideally want good bacteria in your body, to fight off any disease that we might notice. Which means you need to make sure that you have good bacteria in your diet. As you know, autophagy provides you with good bacteria and lots of it. However, it would be best if you made sure that when you have these good bacteria is in your body that you are drinking enough to digest it and to keep your gut healthy.

This is why it is essential that you drink more autophagy which we will talk about that later in this book. However, for now, you need to understand the importance of good bacteria in your body and reducing cancer, overall if your goals to minimize cancer and autophagy will provide you with that. However, if your goal is to reap all the benefits from the autophagy, then you need to make sure that a couple of things are in check before you do so. You need to make sure they get an ample amount of protein, fats, and carbs in your diet. As your diet will be very restricted when it comes to the food you are going to be eating, you need to make sure that you are eating the right macronutrients for your body. This means we need to make sure that you are eating foods that will give you a balanced macronutrient breakdown.

You will be eating no meat, which means you'll have to make up your protein needs are met through plant-based meals and plants-based products. We will give you some fantastic recipes to make good food. However, your goal is to understand that you are hitting the right number of calories for your required body fat on your goals. If you're not eating an ample amount of food, then your body will not have enough energy to fight off these diseases or problems. Which is why you need to understand how many calories you need and eat accordingly based on that. Some people are claiming that you need to be eating enough food regardless of how much or what type of food intake you are following, which means that it is more recommended that you eat enough food to get the optimal results. If you're going through chemotherapy, then you need to be making sure they are eating enough food regardless of what diet you are following. If you want to make sure that your chemotherapy goes successful, then it is crucial that you maintain your weight when you are going through this procedure.

There are some claims made that the autophagy will make it more successful for you when it comes to achieving chemotherapy success. However, many people are claiming this is entirely bogus. No claims are backing up that autophagy helps with chemotherapy. However, many claims are suggesting that the autophagy will help you with reducing the risk of cancer and are getting rid of cancer entirely if you are following the diet. If you talk to your doctor, he or she will tell you that autophagy is one of the best diets to follow when it comes to reducing the risk of cancer. However, this is not the popular answer for most people.

As many people have been brainwashed with media saying that autophagy is not the best way to go about, if the professionals are saying that the autophagy is a great idea, there's some truth behind that. To clarify, there have not been many studies claiming that the autophagy will ultimately help you get rid of cancer. Nonetheless, there have been many real-life situations where this diet has helped.

If you want to make sure that you are getting the best results possible, then make sure that you combine it with a good smoothie routine which will allow you to detoxify your body. It doesn't matter what diet you follow. If you aren't following autophagy or your body is alkaline, then there's a high chance that you will not reduce the risk of cancer. Which means you will be in a much better position following the autophagy when it comes to reducing the risk of cancer, many professionals have claimed as such. One more thing to remember, if you're on acidic medications then you can counteract that with autophagy. Make sure that the medicines that you're taking aren't going to disrupt your autophagy. We can't tell you which medicine will cause you to be acidic, the best way to understand which ones will is to ask your doctor.

To recap, the autophagy will help you keep your body at an autophagy level, which will allow no cancer or bacteria to start activating or to start forming. The autophagy will detoxify you and create new cells which will enable you to fight off cancer and make your immune system even stronger. Moreover, autophagy will also help you with chemotherapy, as many people have said it will. Making this diet a no-brainer to follow. Just make sure that you are eating enough calories to maintain your body weight, especially if you are facing any cancerous diseases. I hope you understand how following the autophagy can help you with reducing the risk of cancer and many other diseases, to clarify there have been no studies showing that the autophagy will help you to get rid of cancer or any other sorts of diseases.

This has been a personal recommendation of many doctors, and an own review of many patients that autophagy has helped them tremendously to reduce the risk of cancer or many other diseases. Which does make sense when you look at the benefits of autophagy. If you're facing any of these diseases, then always consult with your doctor before you start any of this diet. Moreover, as always, know what type of medications you are taking and how you can counterbalance your autophagy. Finally, truly understand what the autophagy is if you have to read this book a couple of times if you are feeling lost.

If you were going to follow this diet blindly, then it would be like riding a bicycle without training wheels. You need to understand the diet before you start following it, and feel it out before you can commit to it. If you can commit to this diet, then you will be in a great position in terms of seeing the benefits. One of the only problems with this diet would be the precise requirements. Also, you cannot drink alcohol or take any particular types of medication when following the autophagy. Make sure they have everything checked before you proceed to follow this diet. Once you have managed to do that, then you will be in a perfect position to start following this diet and to see the benefits of it.

Chapter 7 Recipes

Breakfast

Veggie Salad

Preparation time: 10 minutes

Cooking time: 0 minutes

Servings: 4

Ingredients:
1 red bell pepper, cut into strips

1 green bell pepper, cut into strips

2 spring onions, chopped

1 cup black olives, pitted and halved

1 cup kalamata olives, pitted and halved

A pinch of garlic powder

A pinch of salt and black pepper

1 tablespoon avocado oil

Directions:

In a bowl, combine the bell peppers with the onions and the other ingredients, toss, divide between plates and serve for breakfast.

Nutrition: calories 221, fat 6, fiber 6, carbs 14, protein 11

Sweet Potato and Eggs Mix

Preparation time: 5 minutes

Cooking time: 15 minutes

Servings: 4

Ingredients:

A pinch of salt and black pepper

8 eggs, whisked

1 tablespoon olive oil

1 small yellow onion, chopped

2 garlic cloves, minced

1 cup sweet potato, peeled and cubed

1 cup baby spinach

1 tablespoon chives, chopped

Directions:

Heat up a pan with the oil over medium-high heat, add the onion and the garlic and sauté for 2 minutes.
Add the potato, stir and cook for 3 minutes more.

Add the eggs and the other ingredients, cook for 10 minutes, stirring from time to time, divide between plates and serve for breakfast.

Nutrition: calories 213.3, fat 12.3, fiber 7, carbs 14, protein 2.3

Basil Avocado Salad

Preparation time: 5 minutes

Cooking time: 0 minutes

Servings: 2

Ingredients:

2 avocados, peeled, pitted and roughly cubed
1 mango, peeled and cubed
1 tablespoon lime juice
1 cup baby spinach
Handful basil, torn

1 tablespoon olive oil

¼ cup pine nuts, toasted

A pinch of salt and black pepper

Directions:

In a salad bowl, mix avocados with the mango and the other ingredients, toss and serve for breakfast.

Nutrition: calories 200.1, fat 4, fiber 4, carbs 14.1, protein 5

Brussels Sprouts Eggs

Preparation time: 10 minutes

Cooking time: 15 minutes

Servings: 4

Ingredients:

1 cup Brussels sprouts, shredded

1 yellow onion, chopped

8 eggs, whisked

1 tablespoon olive oil

1 tablespoon turmeric powder

1 tablespoon cilantro, chopped

1 teaspoon cumin, ground

A pinch of salt and black pepper

Directions:

Heat up a pan with the oil over medium-high heat, add the onion and the sprouts and sauté for 5 minutes.

Add the eggs and the other ingredients, toss well, cook for 10 minutes more, divide between plates and serve.

Nutrition: calories 177, fat 2, fiber 6, carbs 15, protein 6

Spinach and Strawberries Bowls

Preparation time: 5 minutes

Cooking time: 0 minutes

Servings: 4

Ingredients:

2 cups baby spinach

10 strawberries, halved

1 tablespoon pine nuts

1 tablespoon almonds, chopped

1 tablespoon lime juice

1 tablespoon avocado oil

Directions:

In a bowl, combine the spinach with the strawberries and the other ingredients, toss and serve for breakfast.

Nutrition: calories 171, fat 3, fiber 6, carbs 15, protein 5

Green Oatmeal

Preparation time: 10 minutes

Cooking time: 20 minutes

Servings: 4

Ingredients:

1 cup old-fashioned oats

1 cup almond milk

½ cup of water

1 tablespoon coconut oil, melted

½ cup collard greens, chopped

½ cup baby spinach, chopped

Handful basil, chopped

½ tablespoon rosemary, chopped

A pinch of salt and black pepper

Directions:

Heat up a pot with the milk and the water over medium heat, add the oats, the oil, and the other ingredients, cook for 20 minutes, stirring often, divide into bowls and serve warm.

Nutrition: calories 246, fat 19.3, fiber 3.8, carbs 17.6, protein 4.1

Quinoa, Greens and Eggs Salad

Preparation time: 10 minutes

Cooking time: 0 minutes

Servings: 4

Ingredients:

1 cup baby spinach

1 cup baby kale

2 spring onions, chopped

2 tablespoons olive oil

1 cup quinoa, cooked

1 carrot, shredded

1 red bell pepper, cut into strips

A pinch of salt and black pepper

1 tablespoon lime juice

4 eggs, hard-boiled, peeled and roughly cubed

Directions:

In a salad bowl, combine the quinoa with the spinach, kale and the other ingredients, toss and serve for breakfast.

Nutrition: calories 308, fat 14.1, fiber 4.4, carbs 34, protein 12.8

Fennel and Barley Salad

Preparation time: 10 minutes

Cooking time: 1 hour

Servings: 2

Ingredients:

1 cup black barley

3 cups of water

2 fennel bulbs, shaved

1 cup baby kale

1 small red onion, sliced

2 tablespoons almonds, chopped

1 avocado, peeled, pitted and cubed

2 tablespoons oil

1 tablespoon pine nuts

2 tablespoons balsamic vinegar

A pinch of salt and black pepper

Directions:

Put the barley in a pot, add the water, salt, and pepper, bring to a simmer over medium heat, cook for 1 hour, drain, cool and transfer to a salad bowl.

Add the fennel, kale and the other ingredients, toss, divide into smaller bowls and serve for breakfast.

Nutrition: calories 545, fat 41.2, fiber 18.1, carbs 42.7, protein 9.8

Chili Sweet Potato Mix

Preparation time: 5 minutes

Cooking time: 20 minutes

Servings: 4

Ingredients:

2 scallions, chopped

2 tablespoons olive oil

4 sweet potatoes, peeled and cut into wedges

1 teaspoon chili powder

1 teaspoon hot paprika

2 carrots, shredded

1 teaspoon sesame seeds

1 tablespoon lime juice

A pinch of salt and black pepper

Directions:

Heat up a pan with the oil over medium heat, add the scallions and sauté for 2 minutes.

Add the sweet potatoes and the other ingredients, toss, cook for 18 minutes more, divide into bowls and serve for breakfast.

Nutrition: calories 371, fat 12.2, fiber 6, carbs 13.1, protein 5

Chives Cucumber Bowls

Preparation time: 5 minutes

Cooking time: 0 minutes

Servings: 4

Ingredients:

2 tablespoons olive oil

2 scallions, chopped

1 tablespoon lime juice

1 tablespoon dill, chopped

3 cucumbers, roughly cubed

2 tablespoons chives, chopped

1 jalapeno, chopped

Handful basil, chopped

1 tablespoon almonds, crushed

1 tablespoon walnuts, chopped

A pinch of salt and black pepper

Directions:

In a salad bowl, combine the cucumbers with the scallions and the other ingredients, toss, divide into smaller bowls and serve for breakfast.

Nutrition: calories 199, fat 4, fiber 8, carbs 15, protein 4

Zucchinis and Barley Mix

Preparation time: 10 minutes

Cooking time: 0 minutes

Servings: 4

Ingredients:

2 zucchinis, cut with a spiralizer

1 cup barley, cooked

2 scallions, chopped

1 tablespoon olive oil

½ teaspoon sweet paprika

A pinch of chili powder

1 tablespoon lime juice

A pinch of salt and black pepper

1 tablespoon oregano, chopped

2 cups baby arugula

½ cup sesame seeds paste

1 tablespoon balsamic vinegar

1 garlic clove, minced

½ teaspoon cumin, ground

Directions:

In a large bowl, combine the zucchinis with the barley, scallions and the other ingredients, toss, divide between plates and serve for breakfast.

Nutrition: calories 226, fat 5, fiber 7, carbs 16, protein 7

Avocado Eggs Mix

Preparation time: 10 minutes

Cooking time: 15 minutes

Servings: 4

Ingredients:

1 avocado, peeled, pitted and cubed

6 eggs, whisked

2 scallions, chopped

1 red bell pepper, chopped

2 tablespoons olive oil

2 garlic cloves, minced

2 eggs, whisked

1 tablespoon cilantro, chopped

Directions:

Heat up a pan with the oil over medium-high heat, add the scallions, garlic and the bell pepper and sauté for 5 minutes.

Add the avocado and the other ingredients, toss, cook for 10 minutes over medium heat, divide between plates and serve.

Nutrition: calories 211, fat 2, fiber 5, carbs 16, protein 5

Coconut Blueberries Mix

Preparation time: 10 minutes

Cooking time: 15 minutes

Servings: 4

Ingredients:

1 cup blueberries

1 tablespoon coconut oil, melted

1/3 cup coconut flakes

1 cup of coconut milk

½ teaspoon nutmeg, ground

½ teaspoon vanilla extract

Directions:

In a small pot, mix the berries with the oil and the other ingredients, toss, simmer over medium heat for 15 minutes, divide into bowls and serve.

Nutrition: calories 208, fat 2, fiber 6, carbs 16, protein 8

Spinach, Cucumber, and Olives Salad

Preparation time: 5 minutes

Cooking time: 0 minutes

Servings: 4

Ingredients:

2 cups baby spinach, torn

2 shallots, chopped

1 cup cucumber, cubed

1 cup kalamata olives, pitted and sliced

1 tablespoon chives, chopped

1 tablespoon balsamic vinegar

A pinch of salt and black pepper

2 tablespoons olive oil

Directions:

In a salad bowl, mix the spinach with the shallots, the cucumber, and the other ingredients, toss, divide between plates and serve for breakfast.

Nutrition: calories 171, fat 2, fiber 5, carbs 11, protein 5

Garlic Sweet Potato Bowls

Preparation time: 5 minutes

Cooking time: 20 minutes

Servings: 4

Ingredients:

2 sweet potatoes, peeled and cubed

1 cup coconut cream

3 garlic cloves, minced

2 tablespoons olive oil

1 yellow onion, chopped

1 teaspoon cumin, ground

1 teaspoon turmeric powder

2 tablespoons parsley, chopped

A pinch of salt and black pepper

Directions:

Heat up a pan with the oil over medium-high heat, add the onion, garlic, cumin, and turmeric, stir and sauté for 5 minutes.

Add the potatoes and the other ingredients, toss, cook for 15 minutes more, divide into bowls and serve for breakfast.

Nutrition: calories 188, fat 2, fiber 8, carbs 10, protein 4

Parsley Cucumber Omelet

Preparation time: 10 minutes

Cooking time: 12 minutes

Servings: 4

Ingredients:

8 eggs, whisked
2 shallots, chopped
A pinch of salt and black pepper
1 cucumber, cubed
1 tablespoon parsley, chopped
1 tablespoon olive oil

Directions:

Heat up a pan with the oil over medium-high heat, add the shallots and sauté for 2 minutes.

Add the eggs mixed with the other ingredients, toss, spread into the pan, cook for 5 minutes, flip and cook for another 5 minutes.

Cut the omelet, divide it between plates and serve for breakfast.

Nutrition: calories 201, fat 2, fiber 5, carbs 11, protein 5

Cinnamon Oatmeal

Preparation time: 10 minutes

Cooking time: 20 minutes

Servings: 4

Ingredients:

2 cups of coconut milk

1 cup old fashioned oats

2 tablespoons flax meal

1 teaspoon vanilla extract

2 teaspoons cinnamon powder

1 teaspoon maple syrup

Directions:

In a small pot, mix the oats with the milk and the other ingredients, toss, bring to a simmer, cook over medium heat for 20 minutes, divide into bowls and serve for breakfast.

Nutrition: calories 454, fat 32.4, fiber 7.6, carbs 35.7, protein 8.5

Hot Broccoli Salad

Preparation time: 10 minutes

Cooking time: 15 minutes

Servings: 4

Ingredients:

1 pound broccoli florets

1 yellow onion, chopped

1 tablespoon olive oil

½ cup coconut cream

1 teaspoon chili powder

1 teaspoon hot paprika

1 teaspoon garlic powder

A pinch of salt and black pepper

Directions:

Heat up a pan with the oil over medium-high heat, add the onion and sauté for 2 minutes.

Add the rest of the ingredients, toss, cook for 12 minutes over medium heat, divide into bowls and serve for breakfast.

Nutrition: calories 153, fat 11.2, fiber 4.5, carbs 12.7, protein 4.4

<u>Minty Greens Bowls</u>

Preparation time: 5 minutes

Cooking time: 0 minutes

Servings: 4

Ingredients:

1 cup spinach, torn

1 cup kale, torn

1 cup black olives, pitted and halved

2 shallots, chopped

1 tablespoon lemon juice

1 tablespoon avocado oil

1 tablespoon mint, chopped

Directions:

In a bowl, mix the spinach with the kale and the other ingredients, toss, and serve for breakfast.

Nutrition: calories 198, fat 6.4, fiber 2, carbs 8, protein 6

Mains

Cabbage Soup

Preparation time: 10 minutes

Cooking time: 35 minutes

Servings: 6

Ingredients:

1 yellow onion, chopped

1 green cabbage head, shredded

2 tablespoons olive oil

5 cups veggie stock

1 carrot, peeled and grated

A pinch of salt and black pepper

1 tablespoon cilantro, chopped

2 teaspoons thyme, chopped

½ teaspoon smoked paprika

½ teaspoon hot paprika

1 tablespoon lemon juice

Directions:

Heat up a pot with the oil over medium heat, add the onion and the carrot and sauté for 5 minutes.

Add the cabbage and the other ingredients, toss, simmer over medium heat for 30 minutes more, divide into bowls and serve.

Nutrition: calories 212, fat 5, fiber 7, carbs 14, protein 12

Sweet Potato and Turkey Soup

Preparation time: 10 minutes

Cooking time: 45 minutes

Servings: 4

Ingredients:

2 tablespoons olive oil

1 yellow onion, chopped

1 green bell pepper, chopped

2 sweet potatoes, peeled and cubed

1 pound turkey breast, skinless, boneless and cubed

1 teaspoon coriander, ground

A pinch of salt and black pepper

1 teaspoon sweet paprika

6 cups chicken stock

Juice of 1 lime

Handful parsley, chopped

Directions:

Heat up a pot with the oil over medium heat, add the onion, the bell pepper, and the sweet potatoes, stir and cook for 5 minutes.

Add the meat and brown for 5 minutes more.

Add the rest of the ingredients, toss, bring to a simmer and cook over medium heat for 35 minutes more.

Ladle the soup into bowls and serve.

Nutrition: calories 203, fat 5, fiber 4, carbs 7, protein 8

Mushroom and Beet Soup

Preparation time: 10 minutes

Cooking time: 40 minutes

Servings: 4

Ingredients:

2 tablespoons olive oil

1 yellow onion, chopped

2 beets, peeled and cut into large cubes

1 pound white mushrooms, sliced

2 garlic cloves, minced

1 tablespoon tomato paste

5 cups veggie stock

1 tablespoons parsley, chopped

Directions:

Heat up a pot with the oil over medium heat, add the onion and the garlic and sauté for 5 minutes.

Add the mushrooms, stir and sauté for 5 minutes more.

Add the beets and the other ingredients, bring to a simmer and cook over medium heat for 30 minutes more, stirring from time to time.

Ladle the soup into bowls and serve.

Nutrition: calories 300, fat 5, fiber 9, carbs 8, protein 7

Chicken Meatball Soup

Preparation time: 10 minutes

Cooking time: 30 minutes

Servings: 4

Ingredients:

2 pounds chicken breast, skinless, boneless and minced

2 tablespoons cilantro, chopped

2 eggs, whisked

1 garlic clove, minced

¼ cup green onions, chopped

1 yellow onion, chopped

1 carrot, sliced

1 tablespoon olive oil

5 cups chicken stock

1 tablespoon parsley, chopped

A pinch of salt and black pepper

Directions:

In a bowl, combine the meat with the eggs and the other ingredients except for the oil, yellow onion, stock, and the parsley, stir and shape medium meatballs out of this mix.

Heat up a pot with the oil over medium heat, add the yellow onion and the meatballs and brown for 5 minutes.

Add the remaining ingredients, toss, bring to a simmer and cook over medium heat for 25 minutes more.

Ladle the soup into bowls and serve.

Nutrition: calories 200, fat 2, fiber 2, carbs 14, protein 12

Lemon Tuna

Preparation time: 6 minutes

Cooking time: 18 minutes

Servings: 4

Ingredients:

4 tuna steaks

1 tablespoon olive oil

½ teaspoon smoked paprika

¼ teaspoon black peppercorns, crushed

Juice of 1 lemon

4 scallions, chopped

1 tablespoon chives, chopped

Directions:

Heat up a pan with the oil over medium-high heat, add the scallions and sauté for 2 minutes.

Add the tuna steaks and sear them for 2 minutes on each side.

Add the remaining ingredients, toss gently, introduce the pan in the oven and bake at 360 degrees F for 12 minutes.

Divide everything between plates and serve for lunch.

Nutrition: calories 324, fat 1, fiber 2, carbs 17, protein 22

Sea Bass with Kale Mix

Preparation time: 10 minutes

Cooking time: 23 minutes

Servings: 4

Ingredients:

4 sea bass fillets, boneless

2 scallions, chopped

2 garlic cloves, minced

2 cups baby kale

2 tablespoons olive oil

1 tablespoon parsley, chopped

Juice of ½ lemon

Directions:

Heat up a pan with the oil over medium heat, add the scallions and the garlic and sauté for 5 minutes.

Add the fish and sear it for 3 minutes on each side.

Add the rest of the ingredients, toss gently, cook everything for 12 minutes more, divide between plates and serve.

Nutrition: calories 204, fat 9.8, fiber 0.8, carbs 3.6, protein 25

Avocado Soup

Preparation time: 10 minutes

Cooking time: 0 minutes

Servings: 4

Ingredients:
3 avocados, pitted and peeled

A pinch of salt and white pepper

1 yellow onion, peeled and chopped

3 cups of water

2 scallions, chopped

1 tablespoon chives, chopped

Directions:

In your blender, combine the avocado with the onion and the other ingredients, pulse well, divide into bowls and serve cold.

Nutrition: calories 200, fat 12.3, fiber 7, carbs 13, protein 7

Asparagus Cream

Preparation time: 10 minutes

Cooking time: 12 minutes

Servings: 4

Ingredients:

1 yellow onion, chopped

1 bunch asparagus, trimmed and chopped

1 tablespoon olive oil

A pinch of sea salt and white pepper

2 garlic cloves, peeled and chopped

2 cups almond milk

½ cup coconut cream

Directions:

Heat up a pot with the oil over medium heat, add the onion and the asparagus and sauté for 5 minutes.

Add the rest of the ingredients, toss, cook everything over medium heat for 7 minutes, blend using an immersion blender, divide into bowls and serve.

Nutrition: calories 191, fat 2, fiber 6, carbs 14, protein 7

Shrimp and Tomato

Preparation time: 10 minutes

Cooking time: 12 minutes

Servings: 4

Ingredients:

3 big tomatoes, cubed

1 pound shrimp, peeled and deveined

2 scallions, chopped

2 spring onions, chopped

2 tablespoons olive oil

1 tablespoon basil, chopped

½ teaspoon garlic powder

A pinch of sea salt and white pepper

1 tables chives, chopped

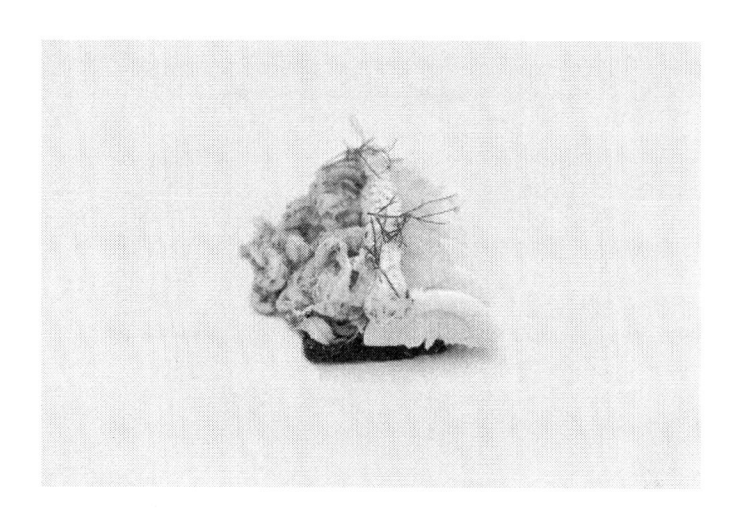

Directions:

Heat up a pan with the oil over medium heat, add the scallions and the spring onions, stir and sauté for 2 minutes.

Add the shrimp and the rest of the ingredients, toss, cook over medium heat for 10 minutes, divide into bowls and serve for lunch.

Nutrition: calories 200, fat 4, fiber 6, carbs 14, protein 9

Almond Salmon Pan

Preparation time: 5 minutes

Cooking time: 16 minutes

Servings: 4

Ingredients:

1 yellow onion, chopped

1 pound salmon fillets, boneless, skinless and cubed

1 tablespoon olive oil

1 tablespoon almonds, chopped

A pinch of salt and white pepper

¼ cup chicken stock

1 tablespoon chives, chopped

Directions:

Heat up a pan with the oil over medium heat, add the onion and sauté for 2 minutes.

Add the salmon and cook it for 2 minutes on each side.

Add the rest of the ingredients, toss, cook everything for 10 minutes more.

Divide everything between plates and serve.

Nutrition: calories 200, fat 11.3, fiber 0.8, carbs 3, protein 22.7

Mushroom Stew

Preparation time: 5 minutes

Cooking time: 30 minutes

Servings: 4

Ingredients:

- 1 yellow onion, chopped
- 1 tablespoon olive oil
- 1 pound white mushrooms, sliced
- 1 cup chicken stock
- 1 cup tomato puree
- 1 carrot, sliced
- 1 teaspoon turmeric powder
- 1 teaspoon chili powder
- ½ teaspoon cumin, ground
- 1 teaspoon coriander, ground
- 2 garlic cloves, minced
- A pinch of salt and black pepper
- 1 tablespoon cilantro, chopped

Directions:

Heat up a pot with the oil over medium heat, add the onion and the mushrooms, stir and sauté for 5 minutes.

Add the carrot and the garlic and cook for 5 minutes more.

Add the stock and the other ingredients except for the cilantro, stir, bring to a simmer and cook over medium heat for 20 minutes.

Divide the stew into bowls, sprinkle the cilantro on top and serve.

Nutrition: calories 199, fat 4, fiber 6, carbs 14, protein 7

Shrimp and Squash Mix

Preparation time: 10 minutes

Cooking time: 12 minutes

Servings: 4

Ingredients:

2 tablespoons olive oil
4 scallions, chopped
1 pound shrimp, peeled and deveined
2 tablespoons pine nuts
1 yellow squash, peeled and cubed
2 garlic cloves, minced
2 tablespoons chives, chopped
Directions:

Heat up a pan with the oil over medium heat, add the scallions and the garlic and sauté for 2 minutes.

Add the shrimp and the other ingredients, toss, cook everything for 10 minutes more, divide into bowls and serve for lunch.

Nutrition: calories 211, fat 6, fiber 4, carbs 11, protein 8

Quinoa and Zucchini Mix

Preparation time: 10 minutes

Cooking time: 20 minutes

Servings: 4

Ingredients:

1 tablespoon olive oil

1 yellow onion, chopped

2 garlic cloves, minced

1 cup quinoa, cooked

2 zucchinis, sliced

1 tablespoon ginger, grated

3 tablespoons coconut aminos

1 teaspoon chili powder

1 teaspoon cumin, ground

1 teaspoon turmeric powder

1 tablespoon hemp seeds

Directions:

Heat up a pan with the oil over medium heat, add the onion and the garlic and sauté for 5 minutes.

Add the quinoa, the zucchinis and the other ingredients, toss, cook everything for 15 minutes more, divide into bowls and serve for lunch.

Nutrition: calories 182, fat 2, fiber 4, carbs 8, protein 11

Chard and Chicken Soup

Preparation time: 10 minutes

Cooking time: 30 minutes

Servings: 4

Ingredients:

1 yellow onion, chopped

2 tablespoons olive oil

2 garlic cloves, minced

1 pound chicken thighs, skinless, boneless and cubed

½ teaspoon turmeric powder

½ teaspoon red chili flakes

A pinch of salt and black pepper

6 cups veggie stock

1 bunch chard, roughly chopped

1 tablespoon cilantro, chopped

Directions:

Heat up a pot with the oil over medium heat, add the onion and the garlic and sauté for 5 minutes.
Add the meat and brown for 5 minutes more.
Add the stock and the other ingredients, toss, bring to a simmer and cook over medium heat for 20 minutes more.
Divide the soup into bowls and serve.

Nutrition: calories 181, fat 4, fiber 4, carbs 9, protein 11

Salmon with Peaches Salad

Preparation time: 5 minutes

Cooking time: 20 minutes

Servings: 4

Ingredients:
1 bunch kale, torn
4 scallions, chopped
2 garlic cloves, minced
1 tablespoon olive oil
A pinch of salt and black pepper
1 cup peaches, cubed
1 pound salmon fillets, boneless and cut into strips
1 tablespoon pine nuts.

1 tablespoon lemon juice

½ tablespoon balsamic vinegar

Directions:

Heat up a pan with the oil over medium heat, add the scallions and the garlic and sauté for 2 minutes.

Add the salmon and cook for 5 minutes more.

Add the rest of the ingredients, toss gently, cook everything for 13 minutes more, divide into bowls and serve for lunch.

Nutrition: calories 211, fat 4, fiber 8, carbs 16, protein 7

Oregano Sea Bass Mix

Preparation time: 5 minutes

Cooking time: 20 minutes

Servings: 4

Ingredients:

4 sea bass fillets, boneless

1 yellow onion, chopped

2 tablespoons olive oil

1 tablespoon lemon juice

1 tablespoon oregano, chopped

2 garlic cloves, chopped

Salt and black pepper to the taste

1 cup cherry tomatoes, halved

1 tablespoon chives, chopped

Directions:

Heat up a pan with the oil over medium heat, add the onion and the garlic and sauté for 2 minutes.

Add the fish and sear it for 2 minutes on each side.

Add the rest of the ingredients, cook everything for 14 minutes more, divide between plates and serve.

Nutrition: calories 273, fat 6, fiber 6, carbs 10, protein 11

Salmon with Horseradish Mix

Preparation time: 10 minutes

Cooking time: 15 minutes

Servings: 4

Ingredients:

1 yellow onion, chopped

1 tablespoon olive oil

1 pound salmon fillets, boneless and cubed

2 teaspoons horseradish

¼ cup coconut cream

A pinch of salt and black pepper

½ teaspoon sweet paprika

1 teaspoon cumin, ground

1 tablespoon chives, chopped

Directions:

4	Heat up a pan with the oil over medium heat, add the onion and the fish and cook for 5 minutes.

5	Add the rest of the ingredients, toss, cook everything for 10 minutes more, divide into bowls and serve for lunch.

Nutrition: calories 233, fat 6, fiber 5, carbs 9, protein 9

Cod with Mustard Sauce

Preparation time: 10 minutes

Cooking time: 15 minutes

Servings: 4

Ingredients:

4 cod fillets, skinless

2 tablespoons mustard

1 tablespoon olive oil

4 scallions, chopped

1 tablespoon capers, drained

A pinch of salt and black pepper

2 tablespoons lemon juice

2 tablespoons cilantro, chopped

Directions:

4. Heat up a pan with the oil over medium-high heat, add the scallions and the capers and sauté for 2 minutes.

5. Add the mustard and the other ingredients except for the fish, whisk and cook for 3 minutes more.

6. Add the fish, cook the mix for 10 minutes, divide between plates and serve.

Nutrition: calories 261, fat 8, fiber 1, carbs 8, protein 14

Salmon with Pineapple Salad

Preparation time: 10 minutes

Cooking time: 0 minutes

Servings: 4

Ingredients:

1 pound smoked salmon, skinless, boneless and cut into strips
2 cucumbers, peeled and cubed
1 pineapple, peeled and cubed
1 tablespoon balsamic vinegar
2 tablespoons olive oil
1 tablespoon cilantro, chopped
A pinch of salt and black pepper

Directions:

In a salad bowl, mix the salmon with the cucumbers, the pineapple, and the other ingredients, toss and serve for lunch.

Nutrition: calories 327, fat 12.2, fiber 1.4, carbs 10. 9, protein 21.9

Seafood

Pecan Crusted Salmon

Preparation time: 20 minutes

Cooking time: 20 minutes

Servings: 6

Ingredients:

3 tablespoons olive oil

3 tablespoons mustard

5 teaspoons raw honey

½ cup chopped pecans

6 salmon fillets, boneless

3 teaspoons chopped parsley

Salt and black pepper to the taste

Directions:

In a bowl, whisk the mustard with honey and oil. In another bowl, mix the pecans with parsley and stir. Season salmon fillets with salt and pepper then place them on a baking sheet, brush with mustard mixture, top with the pecans mix and place in the oven at 400 degrees F to bake for 20 minutes. Divide between plates and serve with a side salad.

Enjoy!

Nutrition: calories 200, fat 10, fiber 5, carbs 12, protein 16

Salmon and Cauliflower

Preparation time: 10 minutes

Cooking time: 25 minutes

Servings: 4

Ingredients:

2 tablespoons coconut aminos

1 cauliflower head, florets separated and chopped

4 pieces salmon fillets, skinless

1 big red onion, cut into wedges

1 tablespoon olive oil

A pinch of sea salt and black pepper

Directions:

Place the salmon in a baking dish, drizzle the oil all over and season with salt and pepper. Place in preheated broiler over medium heat and cook for about 5 minutes. Add coconut aminos, cauliflower and onion then place in the oven and bake at 400 degrees F for 15 minutes more. Divide between plates and serve.

Enjoy!

Nutrition: calories 112, fat 5, fiber 3, carbs 8, protein 7

Salmon and Black Beans

Preparation time: 10 minutes

Cooking time: 30 minutes

Servings: 4

Ingredients:

1 cup canned black beans, drained and rinsed

2 tablespoons coconut aminos

½ cup olive oil

1 ½ cup chicken stock

6 ounces salmon fillets, boneless

2 garlic cloves, minced

1 tablespoon fresh grated ginger

2 teaspoons white wine vinegar

¼ cup grated radishes

¼ cup grated carrots

¼ cup chopped scallions

Directions:

Meanwhile, in a bowl, mix the aminos with half of the oil and whisk. Cut halfway into each salmon fillet, place them in a baking dish and pour the aminos mixture all over. Toss and keep in the fridge for 10 minutes to marinate. Heat up a pan with the rest of the oil over medium heat, add garlic, ginger and black beans. Stir and cook for 3 minutes. Add vinegar and stock, stir, bring to a boil, cook for 10 minutes and divide between plates. Broil fish for 4 minutes on each side over medium-high heat then place a fillet next to the black beans and top with grated scallions, radishes, and carrots.

Enjoy!

Nutrition: calories 200, fat 7, fiber 2, carbs 9, protein 9

Salmon and Roasted Pepper Mix

Preparation time: 10 minutes

Cooking time: 30 minutes

Servings: 4

Ingredients:

3 red onions, cut into wedges

¾ cup green olives pitted

3 red bell peppers, roughly chopped

½ teaspoon smoked paprika

Salt and black pepper to the taste

5 tablespoons olive oil

4 salmon fillets, skinless and boneless

2 tablespoons chopped cilantro

Directions:

Spread peppers, onions, and olives on a lined baking sheet. Add smoked paprika, salt, pepper and 3 tablespoons olive oil then toss to coat. Place in the oven at 375 degrees F and bake for 15 minutes. Rub salmon fillets with the rest of the olive oil, add to the baking sheet and place in the oven to bake for 12 more minutes. Divide everything between plates, sprinkle the cilantro on top and serve.

Enjoy!

Nutrition: calories 301, fat 2, fiber 3, carbs 9, protein 12

Salmon and Black Rice

Preparation time: 10 minutes

Cooking time: 25 minutes

Servings: 2

Ingredients:

½ cup black rice, cooked

2 medium salmon fillets, skinless and boneless

Salt and pepper to the taste

2 teaspoons olive oil

1 garlic clove, minced

12 ounces mixed carrots, tomato, cucumber

1 small mango, peeled and chopped

1 red chili, chopped

1 small piece fresh grated ginger

Juice of 1 lime

1 teaspoon sesame seeds

Directions:

Season salmon fillets with salt and pepper then rub them with oil and garlic. Arrange on a lined baking sheet and place in the oven at 350 degrees F and bake for 25 minutes. In a bowl, mix carrots, tomato, and cucumber with mango, lime juice, rice, ginger, and chili. Mix well then divide between plates, add baked salmon on the side and serve with sesame seeds sprinkled on top.

Enjoy!

Nutrition: calories 220, fat 3, fiber 3, carbs 12, protein 8

Salmon and Coconut Olive Mix

Preparation time: 10 minutes

Cooking time: 12 minutes

Servings: 4

Ingredients:

4 medium salmon fillets, skinless and boneless

1 fennel bulb, chopped

A pinch of salt and black pepper

¼ cup of water

1 cup coconut cream

¼ cup green olives pitted and chopped

¼ cup fresh chopped chives

1 tablespoon olive oil

1 tablespoon lemon juice

Directions:

Arrange the fennel in a baking dish, add salmon fillets and season with salt and black pepper. Add the water and place the mix in the microwave. Cook on High for 12 minutes then divide between plates. In a bowl, whisk the cream with chives, olives, lemon juice, olive oil, salt, and black pepper. Drizzle over the salmon and fennel and serve.

Enjoy!

Nutrition: calories 272, fat 4, fiber 2, carbs 12, protein 7

Mediterranean Coconut Shrimp

Preparation time: 10 minutes

Cooking time: 10 minutes

Servings: 4

Ingredients:

1 cup coconut cream

1 pound shrimp, peeled and deveined

1 tablespoon olive oil

3 garlic cloves, minced

1 tablespoon chopped parsley

¼ teaspoon hot sauce

1 tablespoon lemon juice

½ cup scallions, finely sliced

Directions:

Heat up a pan with the oil over medium-high heat, add the shrimp, toss and cook for 3 minutes. Add the garlic, the hot sauce, lemon juice, and scallions. Mix and cook for 2 minutes more. Add the cream and the parsley then stir, cook for 2 minutes, divide into bowls and serve. Enjoy!

Nutrition: calories 215, fat 3, fiber 2, carbs 8, protein 6

Smoked Salmon and Tomato Mix

Preparation time: 10 minutes

Cooking time: 0 minutes

Servings: 4

Ingredients:

2 tablespoons chopped scallions

2 tablespoons chopped sweet onion

1 ½ teaspoon lime juice

1 tablespoon minced chives

1 tablespoon olive oil

½ pound smoked salmon, diced

1 cup cherry tomatoes, halved

Salt and black pepper to the taste

1 tablespoon chopped cilantro

Directions:

In a bowl, mix the salmon with tomatoes, salt, pepper, chives, onion, scallions, lime juice, oil, and cilantro. Toss well and serve.

Enjoy!

Nutrition: calories 168, fat 7, fiber 3, carbs 17, protein 13

Salmon Salad with Olive Dressing

Preparation time: 10 minutes

Cooking time: 0 minutes

Servings: 4

Ingredients:

FOR THE SALAD DRESSING:

3 tablespoons balsamic vinegar

2 tablespoons olive oil

1/3 cup kalamata olives, pitted and minced

1 garlic clove crushed and finely chopped

Salt and black pepper to the taste

½ teaspoons red pepper flakes, crushed

½ teaspoon lemon zest

FOR THE SALAD:

---

1 pound green beans, blanched and halved

½ pound cherry tomatoes halved

Salt and black pepper to the taste

½ fennel bulb, sliced

½ red onion, sliced

2 cups baby arugula

¾ pound smoked salmon, cubed

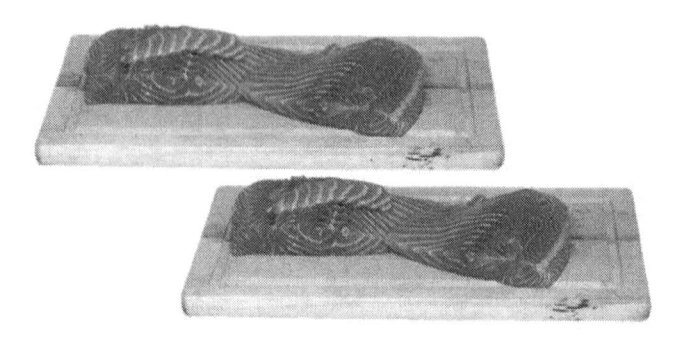

Directions:

In a bowl, whisk the vinegar with garlic, olives, oil, red pepper flakes, lemon zest, salt, and pepper. In a salad bowl, mix the salmon with the beans, tomatoes, salt, pepper, fennel, onion and arugula. Add the salad dressing, toss and serve.

Enjoy!

Nutrition: calories 212, fat 3, fiber 3, carbs 6, protein 7

Mediterranean Shrimp

Preparation time: 10 minutes

Cooking time: 30 minutes

Servings: 4

Ingredients:

1 teaspoon lemon juice

A pinch of salt and black pepper

½ cup avocado mayonnaise

½ teaspoon sweet paprika

A pinch of cayenne pepper

3 tablespoons olive oil

1 fennel bulb, chopped

1 yellow onion, chopped

1 teaspoon orange zest

2 garlic cloves, minced

A pinch of ground cloves

1 cup veggie stock

1 cup canned tomatoes chopped

1 ½ pounds big shrimp, peeled and deveined

¼ teaspoon saffron powder

Directions:

In a bowl, whisk the garlic with the lemon juice, mayo, cayenne, salt, black pepper, 1 tablespoon oil and paprika. Heat up a pan with the rest of the oil over medium-high heat, add onion and fennel, stir and cook for 7 minutes. Add ground cloves, stock, tomatoes, garlic mix, saffron and orange zest then stirs and cook 12 minutes. Add shrimp, stir gently, simmer for 4 more minutes, divide between plates and serve.

Enjoy!

Nutrition: calories 260, fat 2, fiber 5, carbs 8, protein 4

Cod and Endive

Preparation time: 10 minutes

Cooking time: 16 minutes

Servings: 4

Ingredients:

4 cod fillets, boneless and skinless

A pinch of salt and black pepper

Juice of 1 lime

2 endives, shredded

½ teaspoon sweet paprika

1 tablespoon chopped cilantro

1 tablespoon olive oil

Directions:

Heat up a pan with the oil over medium-high heat, add the fish, season with salt and pepper and cook for 3 minutes on each side then divide between plates. Heat up the pan again over medium heat, add shredded endives, salt, pepper, lime juice, and paprika. Toss and cook for 10 minutes then add next to the fish and serve with cilantro sprinkled on top.

Enjoy!

Nutrition: calories 200, fat 2, fiber 4, carbs 10, protein 8

Scallops and Cauliflower Mash

Preparation time: 10 minutes

Cooking time: 15 minutes

Servings: 4

Ingredients:

12 sea scallops

3 garlic cloves, minced

A pinch of salt and black pepper

4 cups chopped cauliflower florets

2 tablespoons olive oil

1 teaspoon chopped rosemary

¼ cup pine nuts, toasted

2 cups veggie stock

2 tablespoons chopped spring onions

Directions:

Put stock in a pot, bring to a boil over medium-high heat, add the cauliflower, bring to a boil, reduce heat to medium, simmer for 10 minutes, drain and transfer to a blender. Add salt and pepper, pulse well then divide between plates. Heat up a pan with the oil over medium-high heat, add rosemary and garlic then stir and cook for 1 minute. Add scallops, salt, and pepper and cook for 3 minutes. Add the next to the cauliflower puree, sprinkle the pine nuts and spring onions on top and serve.

Enjoy!

Nutrition: calories 211, fat 10, fiber 4, carbs 8, protein 14

Citrus Salmon

Preparation time: 10 minutes

Cooking time: 20 minutes

Servings: 8

Ingredients:

3 pounds salmon fillets skinless

A pinch of salt and black pepper

1 tablespoon olive oil

2 oranges, thinly sliced

12 sprigs chopped parsley

Directions:

Season salmon fillet with salt and pepper and arrange in a baking dish. Top with the orange slices, drizzle the oil, sprinkle the parsley and place in the oven at 375 degrees F to bake for 20 minutes. Divide everything between plates and serve.

Enjoy!

Nutrition: calories 210, fat 6, fiber 4, carbs 8, protein 14

Smoked Trout Cakes

Preparation time: 10 minutes

Cooking time: 6 minutes

Servings: 4

Ingredients:

8 ounces smoked trout, skinless, boneless and flaked

Black pepper to the taste

Juice of ½ lime

1 teaspoon sriracha sauce

1 egg white, beaten

1 green onion, chopped

2 tablespoons coconut flour

1 tablespoon olive oil

Directions:

In a bowl, mix the trout with black pepper, lime juice, sriracha, onion, coconut flour, and egg white. Mix well and shape into medium cakes. Heat up a pan with the oil over medium-high heat, add trout cakes, cook for 3 minutes on each side then divide between plates and serve.

Enjoy!

Nutrition: calories 209, fat 15, fiber 6, carbs 8, protein 14

Spiced Salmon

Preparation time: 10 minutes

Cooking time: 10 minutes

Servings: 2

Ingredients:

2 salmon fillets, boneless and skin on

Salt and black pepper to the taste

1 tablespoon ground cinnamon

1 tablespoon coconut oil

Directions:

Heat up a pan with the coconut oil over medium heat, add cinnamon, salt and pepper, and whisk. Add salmon, skin side up, and cook for 5 minutes on each side. Divide between plates and serve with a side salad.

Enjoy!

Nutrition: calories 210, fat 12, fiber 4, carbs 7, protein 14

Scallop and Strawberry Salad

Preparation time: 2 hours

Cooking time: 6 minutes

Servings: 2

Ingredients:

4 ounces scallops

½ cup Pico de gallo

½ cup chopped strawberries

1 tablespoon lime juice

Salt and black pepper to the taste

Directions:

Heat up a pan over medium heat, add scallops, cook for 3 minutes on each side and transfer to a bowl. Add strawberries, lime juice, Pico de gallo, salt and pepper. Toss and serve cold after 2 hours.

Enjoy!

Nutrition: calories 83, fat 1, fiber 1, carbs 5, protein 14

Meat

Pork Chops and Lemon Sauce

Preparation time: 10 minutes

Cooking time: 20 minutes

Servings: 4

Ingredients:

4 pork chops

1 cup pork rinds

1 egg

½ cup coconut cream

2 tablespoons olive oil

½ cup chicken stock

3 tablespoons lemon juice

A pinch of salt and black pepper

2 tablespoons chopped chives

Directions:

In a bowl, whisk the egg with salt and pepper. Put the pork rinds in another bowl. Dip pork chops in egg and then in pork rinds. Heat up a pan with the oil over medium-high heat and add the coated pork chops. Cook them for 4 minutes on one side, flip the place in the oven and cook at 400 degrees F for 10 minutes. Meanwhile, heat up a pan with the stock over medium heat, add the cream, lemon juice, salt, pepper, and chives. Toss and cook for 5-6 minutes and take off the heat. Divide the pork chops between plates and drizzle the lemon sauce over the meat then serve.

Enjoy!

Nutrition: calories 299, fat 7, fiber 5, carbs 13, protein 17

Pork Chops and Blackberry Sauce

Preparation time: 10 minutes

Cooking time: 15 minutes

Servings: 4

Ingredients:

2 pounds pork chops

1 teaspoon ground cinnamon

A pinch of salt and black pepper

12 ounces blackberries

½ teaspoon dried thyme

2 tablespoons water

½ cup balsamic vinegar

A pinch of salt and black pepper

Directions:

Season pork chops with salt and pepper and sprinkle the cinnamon and thyme all over as well. Heat up a small pot with the blackberries over medium heat. Add the vinegar, water, salt and pepper then stir, bring to a simmer and cook for 3-5 minutes. Take off the heat and brush the pork chops with half of this mix. Place the pork on the preheated grill and cook over medium heat for 6 minutes on each side. Divide the pork chops between plates, drizzle the rest of the blackberry sauce all over and serve.

Enjoy!

Nutrition: calories 261, fat 7, fiber 8, carbs 15, protein 16

Grilled Pork Chops

Preparation time: 10 minutes

Cooking time: 25 minutes

Servings: 4

Ingredients:

4 pork chops

A drizzle of olive oil

A pinch of salt and black pepper

½ teaspoon ground cinnamon

½ teaspoon sweet paprika

Directions:

In a bowl, rub the pork chops with salt, pepper, oil, cinnamon, and paprika. Heat up a grill over medium-high heat, add the pork chops and cook them for 2 minutes on each side. Close the grill lid and continue to cook for 20 minutes more. Divide between plates and serve with a side salad.

Enjoy!

Nutrition: calories 251, fat 6, fiber 8, carbs 14, protein 16

Rosemary Pork Chops

Preparation time: 1 hour and 10 minutes

Cooking time: 10 minutes

Servings: 4

Ingredients:

4 pork chops

¼ cup olive oil

2 rosemary springs

Juice of 2 lemons

Zest of 2 lemons

2 garlic cloves

1 teaspoon crushed red pepper

A pinch of salt and black pepper

Directions:

In your blender, mix the oil with the rosemary, lemon juice, lemon zest, garlic, and red pepper and pulse well. In a bowl, mix the pork chops with the rosemary mix, salt, and pepper. Toss well and keep in the fridge for 1 hour. Place the pork chops on your preheated grill, cook for 5 minutes on each side, divide between plates and serve.

Enjoy!

Nutrition: calories 211, fat 4, fiber 4, carbs 15, protein 17

Herbed Pork Chops

Preparation time: 10 minutes

Cooking time: 10 minutes

Servings: 4

Ingredients:

4 pork chops, bone-in

Zest of 1 lemon

3 tablespoons olive oil

Juice of 1 lemon

3 garlic cloves, minced

1 tablespoon chopped thyme

1 tablespoon chopped basil

½ tablespoon ground black pepper

Directions:

In a bowl, mix the pork chops with lemon zest, lemon juice, oil, garlic, thyme, basil, and black pepper. Mix and set aside for 10 minutes to marinate. Heat up your kitchen grill over medium-high heat, add the pork chops and cook them for 5 minutes on each side. Divide between plates and serve.

Enjoy!

Nutrition: calories 251, fat 5, fiber 9, carbs 15, protein 7

Crusted Pork Chops

Preparation time: 10 minutes

Cooking time: 14 minutes

Servings: 4

Ingredients:

4 pork chops, bone-in

2 garlic cloves, minced

3 tablespoons olive oil

A pinch of salt and black pepper

½ cup mustard

Directions:

In a bowl, mix the garlic with the oil, salt, pepper, and mustard and whisk well. Brush the pork chops with this mix and set them aside for 10 minutes. Heat up your grill over medium-high heat, add the pork chops and cook them for 6-7 minutes on each side. Divide between plates and serve.

Enjoy!

Nutrition: calories 194, fat 15, fiber 0, carbs 0, protein 15

Basil Pork Chops

Preparation time: 10 minutes

Cooking time: 12 minutes

Servings: 4

Ingredients:

4 pork chops

2 tablespoons minced garlic

2 tablespoons olive oil

1 cup minced basil

2 tablespoons lemon juice

A pinch of salt and black pepper

Directions:

In a bowl, whisk the garlic with oil, basil, lemon juice, salt, and pepper. Add pork chops and toss them well. Place the chops on the preheated grill over medium-high heat and cook for 6 minutes on each side. Divide between plates and serve.

Enjoy!

Nutrition: calories 261, fat 6, fiber 7, carbs 15, protein 16

Baked Pork Chops

Preparation time: 10 minutes

Cooking time: 25 minutes

Servings: 4

Ingredients:
4 pork chops

2 eggs, whisked

½ cup cashew meal

1/3 cup sunflower seeds, minced

2 teaspoons garlic powder

A pinch of salt and black pepper

1½ teaspoon smoked paprika

1 teaspoon chipotle chili powder

Directions:

In a bowl, mix the cashew meal with sunflower seeds, garlic powder, salt, pepper, paprika, and chili powder. Dip the pork chops in whisked eggs, then in cashew mix and place them on a lined baking sheet and bake at 400 degrees F for 25 minutes. Divide between plates and serve.

Enjoy!

Nutrition: calories 251, fat 12, fiber 4, carbs 7, protein 16

Roasted Pork Chops

Preparation time: 10 minutes

Cooking time: 15 minutes

Servings: 4

Ingredients:

4 pork chops, bone-in

A pinch of salt and black pepper

1 tablespoon olive oil

6 garlic cloves, minced

Directions:

Heat up a pan with the oil over medium-high heat and add the pork chops. Season with salt and pepper and cook for 3 minutes. Flip the pork chops, add the garlic and place in the oven to roast at 400 degrees F for 4 minutes. Divide between plates and serve.

Enjoy!

Nutrition: calories 282, fat 12, fiber 1, carbs 6, protein 17

Skillet Pork Chops

Preparation time: 10 minutes

Cooking time: 25 minutes

Servings: 6

Ingredients:

6 pork chops, bone-in

3 tablespoons olive oil

A pinch of salt and black pepper

¼ teaspoon ground cumin

¼ teaspoon dried rosemary

Directions:

Heat up a pan with the oil over medium-high heat, add pork chops, season with salt, pepper, cumin, and rosemary and cook for 5 minutes on each side. Place the pan in the oven and roast at 350 degrees F for 15 minutes. Divide between plates and serve.

Enjoy!

Nutrition: calories 261, fat 6, fiber 5, carbs 11, protein 18

Cranberry Pork

Preparation time: 10 minutes

Cooking time: 8 hours

Servings: 4

Ingredients:

1 ½ pound pork roast

½ teaspoon fresh grated ginger

1 tablespoon coconut flour

A pinch of mustard powder

A pinch of salt and black pepper

½ cup cranberries

¼ cup of water

Juice of ½ lemon

2 garlic cloves, minced

Directions:

In your slow cooker, mix the roast with the ginger, flour, mustard, salt, pepper, cranberries, water, lemon juice, and garlic. Cover and cook on Low for 8 hours. Slice and divide everything between plates and serve.

Enjoy!

Nutrition: calories 261, fat 4, fiber 8, carbs 9, protein 17

Spicy Pork

Preparation time: 10 minutes

Cooking time: 12 hours

Servings: 6

Ingredients:

6 pork chops

3 chipotle peppers, chopped

¼ cup lime juice

1 small yellow onion, chopped

¼ cup tomato paste

4 garlic cloves, minced

1 ½ tablespoon apple cider vinegar

1 teaspoon dried oregano

2 teaspoons ground cumin

1 cup chicken stock

1 teaspoon cloves

3 bay leaves

Directions:

In your slow cooker, combine the pork chops with chipotle peppers, lime juice, onion, tomato paste, garlic, vinegar, oregano, cumin, stock, cloves and bay leaves. Mix together then cover and cook on Low for 12 hours. Discard bay leaves and cloves then divide the pork mix between plates and serve.

Enjoy!

Nutrition: calories 271, fat 3, fiber 5, carbs 9, protein 16

Vegetables

__Garlic Tomatoes__

Preparation time: 10 minutes

Cooking time: 50 minutes

Servings: 4

Ingredients:

4 garlic cloves, crushed

1 pound mixed cherry tomatoes

3 thyme springs, chopped

A pinch of sea salt

Black pepper to taste

¼ cup olive oil

Directions:

In a baking dish, mix tomatoes with a pinch of sea salt, black pepper, olive oil, and thyme, toss to coat, place in the oven at 325 degrees F and bake for 50 minutes.

Divide tomatoes and pan juices between plates and serve.

Enjoy!

Nutrition: Calories 138, fat 13, fiber 2, carbs 6,6, protein 2

Tomato Quiche

Preparation time: 10 minutes

Cooking time: 20 minutes

Servings: 2

Ingredients:

1 bunch basil, chopped

4 eggs

1 garlic clove, minced

A pinch of sea salt

Black pepper to taste

½ cup cherry tomatoes halved

¼ cup almond cheese

Directions:

In a bowl, mix eggs with a pinch of sea salt, black pepper, almond cheese, and basil and whisk well.

Pour this into a baking dish, arrange tomatoes on top, place in the oven at 350 degrees F and bake for 20 minutes.

Leave quiche to cool down, slice and serve.

Enjoy!

Nutrition: Calories 137, fat 8,9, fiber 0,6, carbs 5,5, protein 13,7

Cumin Cherry Mix

Preparation time: 30 minutes

Cooking time: 4 minutes

Servings: 4

Ingredients:

1 teaspoon coconut sugar

3 cups cherry tomatoes, halved

¼ teaspoon cumin, ground

1 tablespoon sherry vinegar

A pinch of sea salt

1 red onion, chopped

2 cucumbers, sliced

¼ cup olive oil

Black pepper to taste

Directions:

Put cherry tomatoes in a bowl, season with coconut sugar, a pinch of salt and black pepper and leave aside for 30 minutes.

Drain tomatoes and pour juices into a pan.

Heat this up over medium heat, add cumin and vinegar and bring to a simmer.

Cook for 4 minutes, take off the heat and mix with olive oil.

Add tomatoes, onion, and cucumber to this mix, toss well, divide between plates and serve.

Enjoy!

Nutrition: Calories 171, fat 13,1, fiber 3, carbs 14,4, protein 2,5

Zucchini Noodles with Tomatoes and Spinach

Preparation time: 10 minutes

Cooking time: 20 minutes

Servings: 6

Ingredients:

2 tablespoons olive oil

3 zucchinis, cut with a spiralizer

16 ounces mushrooms, sliced

¼ cup sun-dried tomatoes, chopped

1 teaspoon garlic, minced

½ cup cherry tomatoes halved

2 cups marinara sauce

2 cups spinach, chopped

A pinch of sea salt

Black pepper to taste

A pinch of cayenne pepper

Handful basil, chopped

Directions:

Put zucchini noodles in a bowl, season them with a pinch of salt and black pepper and leave them aside for 10 minutes.

Heat up a pan with the oil over medium-high heat, add garlic, stir and cook for 1 minute.

Add mushrooms, stir and cook for 4 minutes.

Add sun-dried tomatoes, stir and cook for 4 minutes more.

Add cherry tomatoes, spinach, cayenne, marinara, and zucchini noodles, stir and cook for 6 minutes more.

Sprinkle basil on top, toss gently, divide between plates and serve.

Enjoy!

Nutrition: Calories 160, fat 8, fiber 4,7, carbs 19,4, protein 5,7

Roasted Tomatoes

Preparation time: 10 minutes

Cooking time: 1 hour

Servings: 4

Ingredients:

1 big red onion, cut into wedges

2 red bell peppers, chopped

2 garlic cloves, minced

1 pound cherry tomatoes, halved

1 teaspoon thyme, dried

1 teaspoon oregano, dried

3 bay leaves

2 tablespoons olive oil

1 tablespoon balsamic vinegar

A pinch of sea salt

Black pepper to taste

Directions:

In a baking dish mix tomatoes with onions, garlic, a pinch of sea salt, black pepper, thyme, oregano, bay leaves, half of the oil and half of the vinegar, toss to coat, place in the oven at 350 degrees F and roast them for 1 hour.

Meanwhile, in a food processor, mix bell peppers with a pinch of sea salt, black pepper, the rest of the oil and the rest of the vinegar and blend well.

Discard bay leaves, divide roasted tomatoes, garlic, and onions on plates, drizzle the bell peppers sauce over them and serve.

Enjoy!

Nutrition: Calories 119, fat 7,5, fiber 3,4, carbs 13,7, protein 2,2

Tomato Skewers

Preparation time: 10 minutes

Cooking time: 6 minutes

Servings: 4

Ingredients:

3 tablespoons balsamic vinegar

24 cherry tomatoes

2 tablespoons olive oil

3 garlic cloves, minced

1 tablespoons thyme, chopped

A pinch of sea salt

Black pepper to taste

Directions:

In a bowl, mix all the ingredients and toss well.

Thread 6 tomatoes on each skewer, place them under a preheated broiler on medium-high heat, broil for 3 minutes on each side and divide between plates.

Serve right away.

Enjoy!

Nutrition: Calories 200, fat 8,5, fiber 9,2, carbs 30, protein 6,7

Veggies and Fish Mix

Preparation time: 10 minutes

Cooking time: 32 minutes

Servings: 4

Ingredients:

1 cup hot water

1 tablespoon maple syrup

2 tablespoons olive oil

1 eggplant, chopped

3 cups cherry tomatoes, halved

1 teaspoon Paleo Tabasco sauce

1 pound tuna, cubed

1 teaspoon balsamic vinegar

½ cup basil, chopped

Black pepper to taste

A pinch of sea salt

Directions:

In a bowl, mix eggplant pieces with a pinch of salt and black pepper and stir.

Heat up a pan with 1 tablespoon oil over medium heat, add eggplant, cook for 6 minutes stirring often and transfer to a bowl.

Heat up the pan again with the rest of the oil over medium heat, add tomatoes, cover pan and cook for 6 minutes shaking the pan from time to time.

Return eggplant pieces to the pan, add maple syrup, vinegar, and hot water, stir, cover and cook for 10 minutes.

Add tuna and Tabasco sauce, stir, cover the pan again, reduce heat to medium-low and simmer for 10 minutes more.

Sprinkle basil on top, divide veggies and tuna mix between plates and serve.

Enjoy!

Nutrition: Calories 395, fat 20,3, fiber 5,7, carbs 15,7, protein 32,8

Spaghetti Squash and Tomatoes

Preparation time: 10 minutes

Cooking time: 50 minutes

Servings: 4

Ingredients:

¼ cup pine nuts

2 cups basil, chopped

1 spaghetti squash, halved lengthwise and seedless

Black pepper to taste

A pinch of sea salt

1 teaspoon garlic, minced

1 and ½ tablespoons olive oil

1 cup mixed cherry tomatoes, halved

½ cup olive oil

2 garlic cloves, minced

Directions:

Place spaghetti squash halves on a lined baking sheet, place in the oven at 375 degrees F and bake for 40 minutes.

Leave squash to cool down and make your spaghetti out of the flesh.

In a food processor, mix pine nuts with a pinch of salt, basil, and 2 garlic cloves and blend well.

Add ½ cup olive oil, blend again well and transfer to a bowl.

Heat up a pan with 1 and ½ tablespoons oil over medium-high heat, add tomatoes, a pinch of salt, some black pepper, and 1 teaspoon garlic, stir and cook for 2 minutes.

Divide spaghetti squash on plates, add tomatoes and the basil pesto on top.

Enjoy!

Nutrition: Calories 324, fat 34,8, fiber 1, carbs 4,9, protein 2,2

Zucchini Noodles and Capers Sauce

Preparation time: 10 minutes

Cooking time: 0 minutes

Servings: 4

Ingredients:

1 tablespoon capers, drained

1 garlic clove

A pinch of sea salt

Black pepper to taste

A pinch of red pepper flakes

15 kalamata olives, pitted

2 tablespoons olive oil

8 ounces cherry tomatoes, halved

Handful basil, torn

Juice of ½ lemon

4 zucchinis, cut with a spiralizer

Directions:

In a food processor, mix capers with a pinch of sea salt, black pepper, pepper flakes, and olives and blend well.

Transfer to a bowl, add basil, oil, and tomatoes, stir well and leave aside for 10 minutes.

Divide zucchini noodles on plates, add tomatoes and capers sauce, toss to coat well and serve.

Enjoy!

Nutrition: Calories 126, fat 9,3, fiber 3,5, carbs 11,3, protein 3,2

Zucchini Noodles and Pesto

Preparation time: 10 minutes

Cooking time: 10 minutes

Servings: 4

Ingredients:

6 zucchinis, cut with a spiralizer

1 cup basil

1 avocado, pitted and peeled

A pinch of sea salt

Black pepper to taste

3 garlic cloves, chopped

¼ cup olive oil

2 tablespoons olive oil

1 pound shrimp, peeled and deveined

¼ cup pistachios

2 tablespoons lemon juice

2 teaspoons old bay seasoning

Directions:

In a bowl, mix zucchini noodles with a pinch of sea salt and some black pepper, leave aside for 10 minutes and squeeze well.

In a food processor, mix pistachios with black pepper, basil, avocado, lemon juice and a pinch of salt and blend well.

Add ¼ cup oil, blend again and leave aside for now.

Heat a pan with 1 tablespoon oil over medium-high heat, add garlic, stir and cook for 1 minute. Add shrimp and old bay seasoning, stir, cook for 4 minutes and transfer to a bowl.

Heat up the same pan with the rest of the oil over medium-high heat, add zucchini noodles, stir and cook for 3 minutes.

Divide on plates, add pesto on top and toss to coat well. Top with shrimp and serve.

Enjoy!

Nutrition: Calories 479, fat 33,7, fiber 7,2, carbs 18, protein 31,5

Stuffed Portobello Mushrooms

Preparation time: 10 minutes

Cooking time: 20 minutes

Servings: 4

Ingredients:

10 basil leaves

1 cup baby spinach

3 garlic cloves, chopped

1 cup almonds, roughly chopped

1 tablespoon parsley

2 tablespoons nutritional yeast

¼ cup olive oil

8 cherry tomatoes, halved

A pinch of sea salt

Black pepper to taste

4 Portobello mushrooms, stem removed and chopped

Directions:

In a food processor, mix basil with spinach, garlic, almonds, parsley, nutritional yeast, oil, a pinch of salt, black pepper to taste and mushroom stems and blend well.

Stuff each mushroom with this mix, place them on a lined baking sheet, place in the oven at 400 degrees F and bake for 20 minutes.

Divide between plates and serve right away.

Enjoy!

Nutrition: Calories 333, fat 25,3, fiber 8,5, carbs 21,1, protein 12,9

Avocado Spread

Preparation time: 10 minutes

Cooking time: 0 minutes

Servings: 4

Ingredients:

2 avocados, pitted and peeled

2 small shallots, peeled, chopped, fried

2 garlic cloves, minced

5 cherry tomatoes, halved

1 jalapeno pepper, chopped

½ red onion, chopped

Juice of ½ lime

A pinch of sea salt

Black pepper to taste

Directions:

Put avocados in a bowl and mash them well.
Add garlic, jalapeno, onion, a pinch of salt, black pepper, lime juice, and shallots and stir well.
Top with cherry tomatoes halves and serve.

Enjoy!

Nutrition: Calories 246, fat 20, fiber 9, carbs 17,9, protein 3,7

Thai Cucumber Noodles and Shrimp

Preparation time: 20 minutes

Cooking time: 5 minutes

Servings: 4

Ingredients:

1 tablespoon Paleo tamari sauce

3 tablespoons coconut aminos

1 tablespoon sriracha

1 tablespoon balsamic vinegar

½ cup of warm water

1 tablespoon honey

3 tablespoons lemongrass, chopped

1 tablespoon ginger, dried

1 pound shrimp, peeled and deveined

1 tablespoon olive oil

For the cucumber noodles:

2 cucumbers, cut with a spiralizer

1 carrot, cut into thin matchsticks

¼ cup balsamic vinegar

¼ cup ghee, melted

¼ cup cashews, roasted

2 tablespoons sriracha sauce

1 tablespoon coconut aminos

1 tablespoon ginger, grated

A handful mint, chopped

Directions:

In a bowl, mix 3 tablespoons coconut aminos with 1 tablespoon vinegar, 1 tablespoon tamari, 1 tablespoon sriracha, warm water, honey, lemongrass, 1 tablespoon ginger, 1 tablespoon olive oil and whisk well.

Add shrimp, toss to coat and leave aside for 20 minutes.

Heat your broiler to medium-high heat, add shrimp, cook them for 3 minutes on each side and transfer to a bowl.

In a bowl, mix cucumber noodles with carrot, ghee, ¼ cup vinegar, 2 tablespoons Sriracha, 1 tablespoon coconut aminos, 1 tablespoon ginger, cashews and mint and stir well.

Divide cucumber noodles on plates, top with shrimp and serve.

Enjoy!

Nutrition: Calories 446, fat 27,4, fiber 1,6, carbs 21,1, protein 29

Veggie Mix and Scallops

Preparation time: 10 minutes

Cooking time: 4 minutes

Servings: 4

Ingredients:

1 cup cauliflower rice, already cooked

1 tablespoon ginger, grated

2 mangos, peeled and chopped

1 cucumber, sliced

2 teaspoons lime juice

½ cup cilantro, chopped

2 teaspoons olive oil

1 and ½ pounds of sea scallops

Black pepper to taste

Directions:

In a bowl, mix cucumber slices with mangos, ginger, lime juice, half of the oil, cilantro and black pepper to taste and stir well.

Pat dry scallops and season them with some pepper.

Heat up a pan with the rest of the oil over medium-high heat, add scallops and cook for 2 minutes on each side.

Divide scallops on plates, add cauliflower rice and mango and cucumber salad on the side and serve.

Enjoy!

Nutrition: Calories 191, fat 4,3, fiber 3,3, carbs 33,3, protein 8,8

Cucumber Wraps

Preparation time: 40 minutes

Cooking time: 0 minutes

Servings: 4

Ingredients:

For the mayo:

1 tablespoon coconut aminos

3 tablespoons lemon juice

1 cup macadamia nuts

1 tablespoon maple syrup

1 teaspoon caraway seeds

1/3 cup dill, chopped

A pinch of sea salt

Some water

For the filling:

1 cup alfalfa sprouts

1 red bell pepper, cut into thin strips

2 carrots, cut into thin matchsticks

1 cucumber, cut into thin matchsticks

1 cup pea shoots

4 Paleo coconut wrappers

Directions:

Put macadamia nuts in a bowl, add water to cover, leave aside for 30 minutes and drain well.

In a food processor, mix nuts with coconut aminos, lemon juice, maple syrup, caraway seeds, a pinch of salt and dill and blend very well.

Add some water and blend again until you obtain a smooth mayo.

Divide alfalfa sprouts, bell pepper, carrot, cucumber and pea shoots on each coconut wrappers, spread dill mayo over them, wrap, cut each in half and serve.

Enjoy!

Nutrition: Calories 313, fat 26, fiber 6,4, carbs 39,4, protein 8,7

Stuffed Peppers

Preparation time: 10 minutes

Cooking time: 40 minutes

Servings: 4

Ingredients:

¼ cup ghee, melted
6 colored bell peppers
1 garlic head, cloves peeled and chopped
10 anchovy fillets
15 walnuts

Directions:

Put the peppers on a lined baking sheet, place under a preheated broiler, cook for 20 minutes and leave them to cool down.

Heat up a pan with the ghee over low heat, add garlic, stir and cook for 10 minutes.

Grind walnuts in a coffee grinder and add this powder to the pan.

Also, add anchovy and stir well.

Peel burnt skin off peppers, discard tops, cut in halves and remove skins.

Divide pepper halves on plates, divide anchovy mix on them and serve.

Enjoy!

Nutrition: Calories 358, fat 31,3, fiber 5,1, carbs 12,9, protein 11,8

Mexican-Style Stuffed Peppers

Preparation time: 10 minutes

Cooking time: 6 hours and 20 minutes

Servings: 4

Ingredients:

4 bell peppers, tops cut off and seeds removed

½ cup tomato juice

2 tablespoons jarred jalapenos, chopped

4 chicken breasts, skinless and boneless

1 cup tomatoes, chopped

¼ cup yellow onion, chopped

¼ cup green peppers, chopped

2 cups Paleo salsa

A pinch of sea salt

2 teaspoons onion powder

½ teaspoon red pepper, crushed

1 teaspoon chili powder

½ teaspoons garlic powder

¼ teaspoon oregano

1 teaspoon cumin, ground

Directions:

In a slow cooker, mix chicken breasts with tomato juice, jalapenos, tomatoes, onion, green peppers, a pinch of salt, onion powder, red pepper, chili powder, garlic powder, oregano, and cumin, stir well, cover and cook on Low for 6 hours.

Shred meat using 2 forks and stir everything well.

Stuff bell peppers with this mix, place them into a baking dish, pour salsa over them, place in the oven at 350 degrees F and bake for 20 minutes. Divide stuffed peppers on plates and serve.

Enjoy!

Nutrition: Calories 395, fat 11,6, fiber 4, carbs 25,9, protein 45,6

Beef Stuffed Peppers

Preparation time: 10 minutes

Cooking time: 55 minutes

Servings: 4

Ingredients:

1 pound beef, ground

1 teaspoon coriander, ground

1 onion, chopped

3 garlic cloves, minced

2 tablespoons coconut oil

1 tablespoon ginger, grated

½ teaspoon cumin, ground

½ teaspoon turmeric powder

1 tablespoon hot curry powder

A pinch of sea salt

1 egg

4 bell peppers, halved lengthwise and seeds removed

1/3 cup raisins

1/3 cup walnuts, chopped

Directions:

Heat up a pan with the oil over medium-high heat, add onion, stir and cook for 4 minutes.

Add garlic, stir and cook for 1 minute.

Add beef, stir and cook for 10 minutes.

Add coriander, ginger, cumin, curry powder, a pinch of salt and turmeric and stir well.

Add walnuts and raisins, stir then take off the heat and mix with the egg.

Divide this mix into pepper halves, place them on a lined baking sheet, place in the oven at 350 degrees F and bake for 40 minutes.

Divide between plates and serve.

Enjoy!

Nutrition: Calories 445, fat 21,7, fiber 3,7, carbs 24,2, protein 40,5

Stuffed Poblanos

Preparation time: 10 minutes

Cooking time: 40 minutes

Servings: 4

Ingredients:

2 teaspoons garlic, minced
1 white onion, chopped
10 poblano peppers, one side of them sliced and reserved
1 tablespoon olive oil
Cooking spray
8 ounces mushrooms, chopped
A pinch of sea salt
Black pepper to taste
½ cup cilantro, chopped

Directions:

Place poblano boats in a baking dish that you've sprayed with some cooking spray.

Heat up a pan with the oil over medium-high heat, add chopped poblano pieces, onion, and mushrooms, stir and cook for 5 minutes.

Add garlic, cilantro, salt, and black pepper stir and cook for 2 minutes.

Divide this into poblano boats, place them in the oven at 375 degrees F and bake for 30 minutes.

Divide between plates and serve.

Enjoy!

Nutrition: Calories 102, fat 4,1, fiber 2,9, carbs 15,6, protein 4,5

Desserts
Cherry Sorbet

Preparation Time: 2 hours and 20 minutes
Servings: 7

Ingredients:

1/2 cup dark cocoa powder

3/4 cup Paleo red cherry jam

1/4 cup maple syrup

2 cups of water

For the compote:

2 tbsp. stevia

1 lb. cherries; pitted and cut in halves

Directions:

In a pan, mix cherry jam with cocoa and maple syrup, stir; bring to a boil, gradually add the water, stir again, remove from heat, leave aside to cool down completely.

Whisk this sorbet again, pour in a casserole and keep in the freezer for 1 hour.

For the compote, mix in a bowl; stevia with cherries, toss to coat and leave aside for 1 hour. When the time has passed, serve this compote with the sorbet.

Nutrition: Calories: 197; Fat: 1g; Fiber: 4g; Carbs: 9g; Protein: 2

Pumpkin Custard

Preparation Time: 1hour 10 minutes

Servings: 6

Ingredients:

1½ cups pumpkin puree

2/3 cup maple syrup

1 cup of coconut milk

2 tbsp. chia seeds ground and mixed with 5 tbsp. water

1 tbsp. baking powder

2 tsp. pumpkin pie spice

A pinch of salt

1 tsp. cinnamon

1/2 tsp. vanilla

Pumpkin seeds for serving

Directions:

In a bowl; mix pumpkin puree with coconut milk, maple syrup, chia seeds mixed with water, baking powder, pumpkin pie spice, a pinch of salt, cinnamon and vanilla and stir well using your kitchen mixer.

Pour this into small ramekins, arrange them on a baking tray filled halfway with hot water, place in the oven at 325 °F and bake for 1 hour.

Take custards out of the oven, leave them to cool down and serve with pumpkin seeds on top.

Nutrition: Calories: 151; Fat: 2g; Fiber: 2g; Carbs: 6g; Protein: 6g

Pumpkin Pudding

Preparation Time: 18 minutes

Servings: 4

Ingredients:

1¾ cup almond milk

1/2 cup pumpkin puree

2 tbsp. tapioca starch

1/4 cup raw honey

1 tbsp. water

1 egg

1 tsp. vanilla extract

1/4 tsp. nutmeg; ground

1/2 tsp. cinnamon; ground

1/8 tsp. allspice; ground

1/4 tsp. ginger; ground

Directions:

In a bowl; mix tapioca starch with water and stir well.

Put almond milk in a pot and mix with honey and egg.

Stir, bring to a boil and stir in the tapioca starch mix. Cook for 2 minutes and take off the heat.

In a bowl; mix pumpkin puree with vanilla extract, nutmeg, cinnamon, allspice, and ginger and stir well.

Pour this into almond milk mix, stir and place over medium-high heat.

Cook for 4 minutes, transfer to dessert bowls and serve after you've chilled in the freezer for 2 hours.

Nutrition: Calories: 246; Fat: 5.3g; Carbs: 43g; Fiber: 0.5; Sugar: 5g; Protein: 6g

Chocolate Parfait

Preparation Time: 2 hours
Servings: 4

Ingredients:

2 tbsp. cocoa powder

1 cup almond milk

1 tbsp. chia seeds

A pinch of salt

1/2 tsp. vanilla extract

Directions:

In a bowl; mix cocoa powder, almond milk, vanilla extract, and chia seeds and stir well until they blend.

Transfer to a dessert glass, place in the fridge for 2 hours and then serve.

Nutrition: Calories: 130; Fat: 5g; Fiber: 2g; Carbs: 7g; Protein: 16g

Avocado Pudding

Preparation Time: 3 hours Servings: 4

Ingredients:

1 cup almond milk
2 avocados; peeled and pitted
3/4 cup cocoa powder
1 tsp. vanilla extract
3/4 cup maple syrup
1/4 tsp. cinnamon

Walnuts chopped for serving

Directions:

Put avocados in your kitchen blender and pulse well. Add cocoa powder, almond milk, maple syrup, cinnamon, and vanilla extract and pulse well again.

Pour into serving bowls, top with walnuts and keep in the fridge for 2-3 hours before you serve it.

Nutrition: Calories: 231; Fat: 8g; Fiber: 5g; Carbs: 7g; Protein: 2.9

Raspberry Popsicles

Preparation Time: 2 hours 15 minutes
Servings: 4

Ingredients:

1½ cups raspberries

2 cups of water

Directions:

Put raspberries and water in a pan, heat up over medium heat, bring to a boil and simmer for 15 minutes.

Take off heat, pour the mix into an ice cube tray, add a popsicle stick in each, introduce in the freezer and chill for 2 hours.

Nutrition: Calories: 58; Fat: 0.4g; Carbs: 0g; Fiber: 2. protein 1.4

Poached Rhubarb

Preparation Time: 15 minutes

Servings: 3

Ingredients:

Juice of 1 lemon

Some thin lemon zest strips

1½ cup maple syrup

4½ cups rhubarbs cut into medium pieces.

1 vanilla bean

1½ cups water

Directions:

Put the water in a pan.

Add maple syrup, vanilla bean, lemon juice and lemon zest.

Stir, bring to a boil and add rhubarb. Reduce heat, simmer for 5 minutes, take off the heat and transfer rhubarb to a bowl.

Allow the liquid to cool down, discard vanilla bean and serve.

Nutrition: Calories: 108; Fat: 1g; Fiber: 0g; Carbs: 0g; Protein: 1g

Passion Fruit Pudding

Preparation Time: 65 minutes

Servings: 6

Ingredients:

1 cup Paleo passion fruit curd

4 passion fruits; pulp and seeds

3½ oz. maple syrup

3 eggs

2 oz. ghee; melted

3½ oz. almond milk

1/2 cup almond flour

1/2 tsp. baking powder

Directions:

Put half of the passion fruit curd in a bowl and leave aside.

In another bowl; mix the rest of the curd with passion fruit seeds and pulp and stir.

Divide this into 6 teacups.

In a bowl; whisk eggs with maple syrup, ghee, the reserved curd, baking powder, milk, and flour and stir well.

Divide this into the 6 cups as well, put them in an oven pan, fill the pan halfway with water, place in the oven at 200 °F and bake for 50 minutes. Take puddings out of the oven, leave aside to cool down and serve!

Nutrition: Calories: 430; Fat: 22g; Fiber: 3g; Carbs: 7g; Protein: 8g

Pomegranate Fudge

Preparation Time: 2 hours 5 minutes Servings: 6

Ingredients:

1/2 cup coconut milk

1 tsp. vanilla extract

1½ cups dark chocolate; chopped

1/2 cup almonds; chopped

1/2 cup pomegranate seeds

Directions:

Put milk in a pan and heat up over medium-low heat.

Add chocolate and stir for 5 minutes.

Take off heat, add vanilla extract, half of the pomegranate seeds and half the of the nuts and stir.

Pour this into a lined baking pan, spread, sprinkle a pinch of salt, the rest of the pomegranate arils and nuts, cover and keep in the fridge for a few hours. Cut, arrange on a platter and serve.

Nutrition: Calories: 68; Fat: 0.9g; Fiber: 4g; Carbs: 6g; Protein: 0.2

Summer Carrot Cake

For the cashew frosting: Preparation Time: 3 hours 15 minutes

Servings: 6

Ingredients:

2 tbsp. lemon juice

2 cups cashews; soaked

2 tbsp. coconut oil; melted

1/3 cup maple syrup

Water

For the cake:

1 cup pineapple; dried and chopped

2 carrots; chopped

1½ cups coconut flour

1 cup dates; pitted

1/2 cup dry coconut

1/2 tsp. cinnamon

Directions:

In your blender, mix cashews with lemon juice, coconut oil, maple syrup, and some apple, pulse very well, transfer to a bowl and leave aside for now.

Put carrots in your food processor and pulse them a a few times.

Add flour, dates, pineapple, coconut, and cinnamon and pulse very well again.

Pour half of this mix into a springform pan and spread evenly.

Add 1/3 of the frosting and also spread.

Add the rest of the cake mix and the rest of the frosting.

Place in the freezer and keep until it's hard enough. Cut and serve.

Nutrition: Calories: 140; Fat: 3.7g; Fiber: 4g; Carbs: 8g; Protein: 4.3

Green Apple Smoothie

Preparation Time: 10 minutes
Servings: 3

Ingredients:

1 big green apple; cored and cut into medium cubes
1 cup baby spinach
1 tbsp. pure maple syrup
A pinch of cardamom
1/2 tsp. cinnamon

1/2 tsp. vanilla extract
Directions:

Put apple cubes in your food processor.

Add spinach, maple syrup, vanilla extract, cardamom, and cinnamon and blend until you obtain a smooth cream. Pour into 2 glasses and serve right away!

Nutrition: Calories: 145; Fat: 0.8g; Fiber: 3g; Carbs: 8g; Protein: 4g

CUPCAKES

Preparation Time: 1 hour 10 minutes
Servings: 6

Ingredients:

16 oz. mulberries; dried

1 tsp. cinnamon; ground

16 oz. dates; pitted and chopped

3 oz. almond butter

3 oz. raw beet juice powder

3 oz. spirulina powder

8 oz. coconut water

1½ cups raw cashews

Directions:

In your food processor, mix mulberries with dates, cinnamon, and butter and blend very well.

Scoop this mix into a cupcake pan and leave aside.

Clean your food processor, mix spirulina powder with half of the cashews and half of the coconut water, blend well, transfer to a bowl and leave aside.

Clean your blender again, add beet powder with the rest of the cashews and the coconut water and pulse well.

Decorate half of the cupcakes with the beets frosting and the other half with the spirulina powder one. Keep cupcakes in the fridge for 1 hour and serve them.

Nutrition: Calories: 340; Fat: 11g; Fiber: 2g; Carbs: 7g;

Carbs: 9g; Protein: 15g

Hazelnut Balls

Preparation Time: 30 minutes
Servings: 4

Ingredients:

10 hazelnuts; roasted

1 cup hazelnuts; roasted and chopped

1 tsp. vanilla extract

2 tbsp. raw cocoa powder

1/4 cup maple syrup

Directions:

Put 1/2 cup chopped hazelnuts in your food processor and blend well. Add vanilla extract, cocoa powder, and maple syrup and blend again well.

Roll the 10 hazelnuts in cocoa powder mix, dip them in the rest of the chopped hazelnuts and arrange balls on a lined baking sheet.

Introduce in the freezer for 20 minutes and then serve them.

Nutrition: Calories: 47; Fat: 2g; Carbs: 11g; Fiber: 0.1; Sugar: 7g; Protein: 2g

Strawberry Cobbler

Preparation Time: 50 minutes Servings: 8

Ingredients:

3/4 cup maple syrup

6 cups strawberries; halved

1/8 tsp. baking powder

1 tbsp. lemon juice

1/2 cup coconut flour

1/8 tsp. baking soda

1/2 cup water

3½ tbsp. coconut oil

A drizzle of avocado oil

Directions:

Grease a baking dish with a drizzle of avocado oil and leave aside.

In a bowl; mix strawberries with maple syrup, sprinkle some flour and add lemon juice.

Stir very well and pour into a baking dish.

In another bowl; mix flour with baking powder and soda and stir well.

Add coconut and mix until the whole thing crumbles in your hands.

Add 1/2 cup water and spread over strawberries.

Place in the oven at 375 °F and bake for 30 minutes. Take cobbler out of the oven, leave aside for 10 minutes and then serve.

Nutrition: Calories: 275; Fat: 9g; Fiber: 4g; Carbs: 9g; Protein: 4

Caramel Ice Cream

Preparation Time: 16 minutes

Servings: 6

Ingredients:

For the caramel sauce:

3/4 cup stevia

1/2 cup coconut milk

2 tbsp. maple syrup

1 tsp. vanilla extract

For the ice cream:

12 oz. firm almond cheese

1 can coconut milk

100 drops liquid stevia

2 tsp. guar

Directions:

In a pan, heat up over medium-high heat 1/2 cup coconut milk, 3/4 cup stevia, and maple syrup.

Stir well, bring to a boil, reduce heat to low and simmer for 3-4 minutes.

Take off heat, add vanilla extract, stir and leave in the fridge to cool down completely.

In your food processor, mix canned coconut milk, almond cheese, a pinch of salt and the caramel and pulse well.

Add guar and blend again well.

Take mix from the fridge and transfer to an ice cream maker. When the ice cream is done, transfer to bowls and serve with caramel on top.

Nutrition: Calories: 161; Fat: 7, fiber 1g; Carbs: 10g; Protein: 3.2

Fruit Jelly

Preparation Time: 10 minutes

Servings: 2

Ingredients:

1 lb. grapefruit jelly

1/2 lb. coconut cream

A handful of fresh berries for serving

A handful nuts; roughly chopped for serving

Directions:

In your food processor, combine grapefruit jelly with coconut cream and blend very well. Add berries and nuts, toss gently, transfer to dessert cups and serve right away!

Nutrition: Calories: 70; Fat: 29g; Carbs: 4.4g; Fiber: 1g; Protein: 3.5; Sugar: 1

Conclusion

Autophagy is not easy as we would like it to be, but with the current knowledge of how it is stimulated, there are lifestyle practices that at least wouldn't hurt to attempt. The caution to all this is that we don't want these processes to be on or off all the times and we certainly don't want to be in a catabolic state.

Keep in mind that when it comes to this method, you have to make sure that your diet is perfect or at least good to see results. As you read this book, we talked about intermittent fasting and how it can help you to see your results from autophagy. Also, a Ketogenic diet can help you tremendously with autophagy.

You are keeping that in mind, it is now in your hands to decide what kind of diet you're going to be following and how you're going to get there based on the knowledge provided to you in this book. What we did a great job in this book was to help it be more customized. More specifically, how to figure out how to pick out the right plan for your needs and how to achieve the true autophagy that you have been looking for.

Printed in Great Britain
by Amazon